FROM MISTAKES TO MIRACLES

FROM MISTAKES TO MIRACLES

A Jewish Birthmother's Story of Redemption, Hope, and Healing

BY LORI PRASHKER-THOMAS

Author's Note: This is a work of nonfiction, based on memories and historical documents. Some names have been changed for privacy.

Acknowledgments

Writing a book about the story of your life is a surreal process and more challenging than I ever imagined. None of this would have been possible without my amazing husband, Michael. He stands by me during every struggle and all my successes—true love at its best.

To my Mom and Dad (Of Blessed Memory): Thank you for loving me when I did not love or even like myself, and for pushing me to do better!

To my family: Thank you for supporting me through this process. I am so thankful to have you ALL back in my life.

To my chosen family (and there are many of you): Thank you for being there for me and supporting me in this venture and for your love and support in life itself.

To N&A: I am incredibly thankful for everything you have done— including making sure "Olivia" had a lasting relationship with family, encouraging her to spend time outside, sending her to camp and college, giving her a sense of humor, teaching her that with freedom comes responsibility, and for instilling a deep love for the Detroit Red Wings.

To QML: Thank you for supporting my ventures (and there are plenty!) and guiding me accordingly. I could not ask for a better person to work for and with.

To PC: Thank you for listening, and for your guidance, and friendship! I would not ever have taken the first step without your words of encouragement.

To my circle of friends (small as it may be, but you know who you are): Thank you for pushing me to write, keeping tabs on me with my writing goals and word counts, and listening to my frustrations!!!

To A.S. Thank you for your help and support throughout this journey. I could not have done any of this without you.

Finally, to all who have been a part of this journey, whether big or small, thank you!

Thanks.

Chapter 1

The cool wind tousled the fronds of the palm trees just outside my Florida window. Two blocks away, on the edge of the beach town where I had run from all my problems, the surf sprayed rhythmically onto the beach. The gulls whined as they wheeled through the sky, looking for food.

But here in my drab gray apartment in the middle of Delray Beach, my heart was anything but cheery. I let my tousled head sink into the cushion on my couch. Grabbing another pillow, I smashed it against my ears, trying to block out my partner Kito's words that still rang in my ears.

"You're cheating on me, you worthless woman!"

Yesterday, the phone had rung in our apartment, and my then-husband, Kito, hadn't recognized the number.

"Who was that?" he'd demanded.

"It was just someone who had a wrong number," I tried to convince him.

But he would not believe me. "I swear you're having an affair."

Now, bruises covered my body, memories of last night's abuse. Finger-shaped lines tangled across my neck where he had grasped me and tried to strangle me.

Tears of desperation wet the pillow. Behind me, I could vaguely hear my eight-month-old, Ruby, howling in lonely fear. Her curls were sweaty, stuck against her beautiful rich brown cheeks. I continued to sob.

What can I do? Should I tell my parents what bad shape I'm in? No, I can't do it.

I had secrets that my devout Jewish parents and sisters didn't know about. They didn't know I was married. They didn't know I'd given birth to my beautiful biracial baby, Ruby. And they certainly didn't know about a tiny, fair-skinned girl that I had placed for adoption just two short years ago.

How could I tell them now? How could I let them know I was desperate, abused, and alone—when they didn't even know the basic facts about my life?

On the floor around me lay a heap of unfolded laundry. Ruby snuffled, her face crusty with snot. Post-partum depression had never really left me since the day I walked out of the hospital without my first daughter. Now, with a second baby, I could not handle anything emotionally.

I have no one to talk to and nowhere to turn, I thought in despair. *I don't want to live anymore.*

The first two times I had attempted suicide, I hadn't succeeded. I had been young, and I hadn't really known what I was doing. This time, I would do my research.

I'm not going to have another failed attempt, I thought. *This time I am going to slash my wrists. I am not going to live this life any longer.*

I made sure Ruby was safe in her playpen where her dad would find her when he walked in after work. I planted one last kiss on her black curls, turned resolutely, and walked away. Closing the door to the bathroom, I prayed the traditional Kaddish prayer that Jewish mourners pray over their dead loved ones. I wasn't sure that anyone would care enough to pray it over me.

"May there be abundant peace from heaven, with life's goodness for us and for all thy people Israel. And let us say: Amen."

Minutes later, as blackness seeped over my field of vision, I felt relief. Finally, I could slip away from the blackness that was my life.

But apparently, G~d had another plan for me. I lived.

I came back to consciousness a few minutes later, still alive. The throbbing pain in my wrists matched the pain in my heart. My head ached with fear and regret. Questions started shooting through my mind.

How did I get here?

How did I end up with blood dripping from my wrists, unable to tell anyone about the secrets weighing so heavily on my heart?

Why do I feel so worthless?

Maybe G~d did still have a plan for me, one filled with "abundant peace from heaven, with life's goodness for us and for all thy people Israel." But before I would understand this peace and goodness, I would have to take a long, lonely path of self-examination. It would take me a long time before I would finally find hope.

Why did I devalue my own worth as a Jewish Birthmother? Why did I see myself as worthless that lonely afternoon? To truly answer this question, we will need to go all the way back to my childhood.

* * *

My family and I sat around the Seder table, a place of tradition, peace, and unity. The candle flickered over my seven-year-old face. My sisters reverently tasted the bitter herbs, reminding us of the bitterness of slavery.

I gazed at my mother's gentle doe eyes, illuminated by candlelight. Father's slender hooked nose cast a long shadow over the side of his face. His voice rang out loud and clear as he read about the deliverance the L-rd had promised His people:

"When the L-rd will return the exiles of Zion… our mouth will be filled with laughter, and our tongue with joyous song… Those who sow in tears will reap with joyous song. He goes along weeping, carrying the bag of seed; he will surely come [back] with joyous song."

I gazed hopefully at the cup for Elijah, which waited by his empty spot at the table. It was a reminder of our quiet hopes that *this* was the year that the messiah's forerunner would appear to deliver us. The extra cup for Elijah was a symbol of hope and redemption.

I sipped another cup of grape juice. I could tell my sisters, who were drinking real wine, were already beginning to feel the jovial euphoria of drinking four cups of wine in one night. I nibbled the dry, comforting taste of Matzah.

The entire night was filled with special symbolism. The afikomen, the piece of unleavened bread, was wrapped in a napkin and hidden. We'd looked in all the best places: on the bookshelf, behind a picture on the wall, in the mailbox, under the tablecloth. Finally, we found it in the dryer!

The lost had been found. The broken had been healed. The oppressed had been delivered. These family traditions were markers of safety and peace.

As the night wrapped up, already "shnookered" from the four cups of wine, we laughed our way through "Chad Gadya." This song was our Jewish version of "the old lady who swallowed the fly" or "the house that Jack built." It was a lighthearted Hebrew cumulative ditty that built upon itself, verse by verse, until verse ten read,

> "Then came the holy One, Blessed be He,
>
> And smote the angel of death,
>
> Who slew the slaughterer,
>
> Who killed the ox,
>
> That drank the water,
>
> That put out the fire,
>
> That burned the stick,
>
> That beat the dog,
>
> That bit the cat,
>
> That ate the goat,
>
> Which my father bought for two zuzim.
>
> One little goat,
>
> One little goat."

One final giggle, one final flicker of the candle, and our beautiful evening drew to a close.

Growing up, my mother was very kind and nurturing. Even though she often felt depressed and was in pain from arthritis, she did her best to take care of me. When I was sick, she'd bring me steaming bowls of rich chicken broth or Matzo ball soup, with dumplings of Matzah and chicken fat. I snuggled my blanket against my cheek, sipped the flavorful broth, and yawned with relief. Mom touched my cheek.

"Get some rest, Lori," she said. "Later this afternoon, I'll check on you and we can read a story together."

I loved it when Mom read to me. On rainy afternoons, Mom and I would do arts and crafts together. She was an artist and photographer, and she passed on her love of art to me. Mom was gentle and tender to me, trying to compensate for dad's habitual stoicism.

Dad made up for his lack of emotion in other ways. My dad and I would play card games or Rack-o. He was brilliant, and it was nearly impossible to win against him. I loved the evenings Dad and I spent playing games, or watching Dad play bridge with my grandmother. I later found out, to my surprise, that Dad was ranked in playing bridge!

Other days, we'd sit together and watch TV. At night, my dad would watch Wheel of Fortune and then Jeopardy. He tried out for Jeopardy three times; he knew the answers, but his reflexes weren't fast enough.

On Saturday afternoons, I would watch American Bandstand, and my sisters would join in. I remember sitting in front of the television, totally engrossed in the show. I carefully watched all the dancers, then stood up and imitated their dance moves. After I had seen a dance one time, I could repeat the entire dance.

"Lori, you are so good at dancing!" Mom marveled, and she signed me up for a dance class. Over the years, my love of dance only continued to grow.

We also loved watching the New York Giants.

"If you don't root for the Giants, you don't eat," Mom joked. I became a true fan—win or lose, good season or bad season.

In our home, broken things were fixed immediately. Dad always tinkered with broken light fixtures, plumbing, and even the radio. He'd take the item apart and lay all the pieces out, puzzling intently on how to put them back together.

"Dad can take anything apart, but he can't necessarily put it back together again," we'd tease him affectionately.

He was very good at telling you how to fix something, but couldn't necessarily do it himself. I would later inherit his talent... the propensity to tell you when something was wrong or wasn't working properly—yet having no idea how to fix it.

Chapter 2

My family was accepting and kind, and I felt loved within my household. But in other areas of my life, I felt very alone. As soon as I walked outside the four walls of my childhood home, I felt like a vulnerable outcast.

I attended a small Orthodox Jewish Elementary school in Northeastern Pennsylvania. To say small is an understatement. There were eight children in my graduating class. Because of how small my class was and how relatively small the Jewish community was, I was with the same people in school and during the summers at the Jewish Day Camp. I never got a break from them. And since I was an outcast, being stuck with the same people, day in and day out, year after year, seemed like an emotional death sentence.

On the one hand, it was hard to understand why I was bullied. I was Jewish, just like the rest of them. I came from a stable family and looked like everyone else. Plus, I was kind and flexible and always tried my best to get along with people. Yet the kinder and more flexible I tried to be, the more they pounced on my anxiety.

I dreaded gym class. The teacher would make us run laps, dribble basketballs, and shoot baskets. I never seemed to be as alert and agile as the other girls. The girls picked on me, and Sara was the ringleader.

One day, we were playing volleyball. I was desperately watching the ball as it zoomed back and forth between the players. When it came in my direction, I frantically whizzed my arms through space, hoping against hope that I would feel the smooth *whack* of the ball against my forearms. But instead, it whished to the ground to my left.

"Lori!" the girls shrieked in disappointment.

Sara angled her body in my direction and hissed each word through clenched teeth: "You are worthless."

My head dropped in shame, but I clenched my hands together and held my arms out, showing them I was ready for the next ball. When the game started up again, I was furiously leaping back and forth, desperately hoping to please my antagonists.

"Look at her go!" they mocked.

I sank to the ground and sipped from my water bottle. No matter how hard I tried, it was always useless.

One afternoon, I sat alone in my room, hunched over my school science project. The teacher's words echoed in my mind: "After school tonight, make sure you call your friends and ask them to help you with the project. Remember, this is a *group project.* I won't take individual work."

Calling my classmates was the last thing I wanted to do. I dreaded the answer I feared I would get from them: "Go work on your dumb project by yourself. We don't want you on our team."

But that can't happen, I reasoned with myself, trying to gather the courage to lift the phone receiver. *They have to let me help. After all, the teacher said it is a group project. They can't say no to me.*

With that reassurance, I punched the numbers and fiddled anxiously with the phone cord. While the phone started ringing, my heart was pounding. I wanted to slam the phone back in its cradle, but instead, I kept listening until I heard the voice of my friend's mom. I could hear the giggles of girls in the background.

My classmates are already at her house, working, I thought. *I called the right person!*

"Hi Mrs. P," I said. "I'm calling to ask Sara if I can come over and work on the school project.

"Sara!" I heard the mom say, barely covering the receiver. "Your friend from school wants to come over and work on the group project."

"Which friend? All my friends are already here."

"Lori."

I could hear the voices in the background.

"Oh *her?* She's not my friend."

"I don't want her to come over!"

"She's disgusting, I don't want her around."

My heart sank, pounding furiously.

The next day, fear struck me like a sledgehammer. In class, my stomach was in knots. The teacher was reading aloud a short story, "Pearl," by Steinbeck, but I could barely focus. The teacher noticed my glazed eyes.

"Lori, what did we just read about?"

My heart pounded. What could I say? I *was* listening, but the words just didn't make sense.

"Uh…" I stuttered.

The class snickered.

"See? She never listens," Sara whispered.

"Lori, please pay more attention next time," said Mrs. T. She called on someone else.

On the inside, I felt like I was dying. I knew the real reason I was being bullied.

It's because I'm dumb.

I tried to hide from everyone that I had a learning disability. But they noticed. When Dr. M would pull me out of the classroom, the other children would giggle.

"We're going to have a fun time learning together," Dr. M told me on the way to the small classroom where we had our one-on-one class. She was trying to make it sound light-hearted and normal. But I was dying inwardly. I knew the truth. In a few minutes, I would be seated at a desk in a small room with Dr. M. Just like it did every day, my chest would soon fill with the warm, heavy feeling of shame. I would press my finger against the page and stumble over the words in the reader.

After I read the passage, Dr. M would ask me questions to see if I understood. And just like every day, I would look back and forth in desperation, trying to find clues about what the passage had said and what it had meant. Reading comprehension was not my strong suit.

Now, fear flooded me as I dragged my feet and followed Dr. M.

I'm dumb, I thought. *I will never be smart like the rest of them.*

And on the playground, my classmates confirmed my worst fears.

"She's stupid," they taunted.

"You're trash."

"You have no friends."

At home, I wilted. I ran to my room, closed the door, and sobbed. My family knew that my room was my safe place. Whether the door was open or closed, they knew they should leave me alone. In our family, each person's room was their own personal space. Unless a family member was in the common areas of the house, or unless they called another person into their bedroom, their privacy was respected.

My room was a welcoming place. The floors were smooth linoleum, unlike the other carpeted rooms in the house. There was a closet on the left, and a dresser to the right. On one wall, there was stylish brown paneling. On the other wall, cheery clown paintings smiled down at me. A long desk stretched against the wall, and behind it was the window that faced outward into the crisp beauty of the East Coast. It was a wonderful place, and I knew I was safe there.

But none of this brought me any comfort on this particular day. I lay on my bed feeling broken. After I had sobbed alone for a long time, I finally called my mother into my room.

"The kids at school hate me," I cried into her warm, soft arms.

Mom sat in my room and let me talk and cry for as long as I wanted to.

"It doesn't matter what everyone else thinks," she crooned, smoothing back the sweaty hair from my forehead. "You are who you are, and we love who you are."

Mom tried to help me as much as she could. The rest of the evening, she checked on me and showed me her love and support. She tried as hard as she could to fix things. But there were some things she could not fix.

The next morning, I was still in the same predicament.

"I don't want to go to school," I complained to my mother. "My stomach hurts… I have a headache."

It was true that my anxiety had caused tension headaches and tied my stomach up in knots. But it was also true that I was desperate. I would say or do anything so that my mother would keep me home from school.

"You have to go to school to learn," Mom said, looking at me with kind, sad eyes. And with that, she sent me to school anyway.

Mom and Dad had placed us in our Jewish school for a reason, and there was no possibility of moving me to a school where I would be treated better. My mother was raised in an Orthodox Jewish home and my father was raised in a Reformed Jewish home. When they got married, they compromised and raised their family in a conservative shul but educated us in an orthodox elementary school.

My mom felt that schooling was very important. She wanted us to at least have the basic background of orthodox teaching. She knew she couldn't teach us herself, so my sisters and I all went to a very small school. There was no option to transfer me to another school. So with a sinking feeling in my stomach, I walked back into the lions' mouths.

That day at school, the bullying didn't stop. My depressing thoughts just continued to swirl, like a dark cloud. I finally decided to go talk to the teacher.

"Everyone hates me," I said.

"Ignore it and it will stop," she would reply.

Later, I decided to try talking to the school counselor.

"My classmates are bullying me," I said to the counselor.

"You need counseling because it's your fault you have no friends," she replied heartlessly.

When I complained to the principal, he replied, "You brought it on yourself."

Ashamed and miserable, I asked myself, "How did I bring this on by being me?" But no matter how many times I pondered this question, I couldn't understand the answer.

Though the bullying never stopped, and I did not enjoy my education, I did learn something. My sisters and I learned the basics of reading and praying in Hebrew. With our rudimentary grasp of Hebrew, we could go into any shul and daven without an issue and read Chumash verses and translate Rashi. With the Jewish education I received, I learned the duties of my religion. I went to the temple most weeks and did what I was supposed to do.

During the summers, we went to a Jewish camp, as well. My parents sent me to JCC camp so I could grow in Jewish identity, faith, and community in an immersive setting with good role models, connection, and laughter. I loved jumping into the pool and participating in drama and dance. But most of all, I loved the opportunity to spend long afternoons inside the art building.

This particular afternoon in 1984, it was pouring rain. I spent all day in the art building: stroking the smooth, wet ceramic mud into just the right shape, spreading colorful paints over my canvas, and expressing myself in a calm, quiet atmosphere where I could talk in low voices to my friends and counselors.

That night, the rain had not let up. As we settled down in our tents for the night, I could see the rivulets of water running down the sides of the tent. Rain continued to pummel us in sheets. It seeped through the floor of the tent and soaked my sleeping bag and my foam rubber pillow. It was difficult to sleep, and I was grateful when the pink sun peeked through the rustling leaves of the trees.

That afternoon, when I got home, I lugged my musty, wet sleeping bag into the house. I stuffed the bag, the pillow, and my pajamas into the dryer and pressed start. Then I jumped into the shower to wash off the mud, sweat, and grime that had accumulated over a weekend in the rain.

I hadn't even finished my shower when my mom came storming into the bathroom.

"What did you put in the dryer?!?!" she yelled.

"My pillow and sleeping bag," I said through the sound of water.

"Get out of the shower and get dressed—the dryer is smoking!"

I jumped out of the shower, eyes wide with alarm. I was beginning to smell the strong stench of burning rubber. Getting dressed and running to the hall, I saw that smoke was pouring out of the laundry room. Black smoke billowed out of the entire half of the house where the dryer was consuming my now-melted rubber pillow.

"Fire!" I heard someone scream.

I barely had time to glance toward the laundry room. But a flash of fear erupted in my mind. I knew the truth: *This is my fault.*

I ran outside as fast as I could and stood shivering on the lawn. Our neighbor was shouting at the family members who were still inside.

"Get out! The fumes are so bad!"

The sickening feeling in the pit of my stomach only deepened as I watched the flames grow. The laundry room was quickly turning into a pile of ashes. The words took form in my mind:

My rubber pillow caused all this. I should have known! You can't put pillows in the dryer! What have I done? It's all my fault!

Chapter 3

Days later, we sorted through the remains of our family's possessions. Everything was covered in a thick, black dust that destroyed our keepsakes and ate the gold paint off of the baby grand piano strings. We stood in silence and surveyed all that was left of our family's memories.

Tears escaped from the corner of my mom's eye as she looked through the photo albums. There wasn't much left of them except the metal coil of one of the older photo books and the ring binders of the newer ones.

"Our wedding…" I heard her murmur.

Years and years of family history had gone up in smoke. And it was all my fault.

After the fire, we were out of our house for about two years while we fought with the insurance company to pay for the rebuilding of the house. We moved into temporary housing while we waited for the insurance to decide to repay it.

One day, we all sat in the beautiful, ample living room in the apartment we were renting. Outside our room, a balcony looked down over a spacious rotunda. Marble pillars, fragrant hydrangeas, and exquisite ironwork complemented the large lobby.

But inside, we were drowning in details. Mom and Dad sat on opposite sides of the round table, looking through the pile of insurance paperwork once again to see if they could find a loophole. Mom sighed.

"Insurance is really putting up a fight," Dad answered her unspoken frustration, shuffling again through the papers in front of her.

Deep down, even at twelve, I knew the reason insurance wouldn't pay: *The fire was caused by a family member.*

"It was all my fault," I murmured, hanging my head in shame.

"Lori." Mom's voice was firm and loving. "It was an accident."

"But I could have known better. It couldn't have been a complete accident because I should have known that pillows can't go in the dryer—only bedding and sheets."

"Lori, I want you to get the dictionary right now and look up the word, 'accident,'" Mom commanded.

I sighed and reluctantly dragged myself to the bookshelf. I pulled off the tattered red New College Edition dictionary. In bright gold print on the spine, it read, *"AMERICAN HERITAGE DICTIONARY."* Thankfully, some of the books and dictionaries had been salvaged from our house, even though almost all of our precious family photos had gone up in smoke.

Fingering through the filmy pages, I found the spot.

"An unforeseen event that is not the result of intention," I read aloud.

"Did you foresee this event?" Mom quizzed.

"No."

"Did you intend it to happen?"

"No."

"All right then. Now on to the next dictionary."

"Mom…"

We had a lot of dictionaries, because my father loved crossword puzzles and even entered crossword puzzle contests. But Mom made me look up the word "accident" in every single dictionary we had.

"But we lost all the photos," I mourned after I closed the last dictionary.

"We will do what we can to replace them," Mom said. "We've sent photos to relatives, and they may be able to give them back. Think of it, Lori! Your sisters have photos, and so do your aunts and your grandparents. Don't worry, we'll find a way to replace the photos."

In the end, we did get some replacement photos. But the pictures of mom and dad's wedding were lost forever. We couldn't find a single photograph of their wedding. Mom's dress, the cake, the loving moments of gazing into each other's eyes—all of it was gone forever.

After the fire, when we rebuilt the house, everything we had left gained extreme importance. We realized that we could take nothing for granted: neither physical things like photos nor nonphysical things like life and family. We treasured the photos we still had. They captured those moments in time that would otherwise be lost forever.

My mom always used to say, "People are important, things can be replaced." Having the fire in our house made us realize she was one hundred percent right. But we also realized how important it was to treasure the physical items, the photos, and the mementos that weaved us together as a family. And no physical item was as important as the blessing of being together as a family.

When we moved back into the house, I got to choose my bedroom. I picked the last bedroom in the hallway. It was the smallest bedroom, but it was the room I had always wanted. I adored that back bedroom because it overlooked our backyard. In summer, the trees out the window were lush and beautiful. In winter, the snow on the gently sloping yard was dazzling.

As we rebuilt, I picked out all the furniture and décor according to my tastes. I chose purple shag carpet, very 80s, and modern furniture, all mirrored. I loved the modern, contemporary style. There was a nightstand and a walk-in closet. My bed was against the wall, next to the window. In this way, I could spend time gazing outside at the beautiful view. I absolutely fell in love with that room.

Though my physical home was rebuilt, my inner world was still very much in shambles. Even in my spectacular new room, I still spent a lot of time crying on my bed.

The remainder of my eighth-grade year only got harder from there. I was bullied and harassed daily in school and at summer day camp. Towards the middle of my eighth-grade year, when I was thirteen years old, I got very ill and had to have surgery. A few days later, when I returned to school, I was picked on for having to have surgery.

"You are lying about your surgery," one of my classmates said to me. "I wish you had died in that surgery. You are nothing anyway and no one would care whether you lived or died."

That afternoon, I received a letter from a classmate. When I opened it up, fear and shock flooded my body. Words jumped off the page at me:

"You are nothing...a nobody...

"...a useless piece of trash...

"…a child that should never have been born."

Well, that was it for me. I had had enough. I went home that night, knelt on my purple shag carpet, and sobbed in despair.

In huge gulps, I swallowed all the painkillers I had. But there were not enough in the bottle to end my life. When I realized I was still alive, I sobbed with hopelessness.

My parents took me to the hospital, but I was quickly released.

"You need to see a psychiatrist," the hospital confirmed.

Despite my struggles, I returned to school and finished out the year very unhappily. Those words from my classmate never left me; they accompanied me throughout the entire school year and stuck with me into adulthood. When I'm not careful, those words still resonate in my soul even now.

I had no idea how many more hurtful words would be spoken to me—or how I would finally decide to speak up so that other women in my shoes would receive the dignity and support they deserve.

As I recovered from that incident, Mom continued taking care of me and cheering me up as best she knew how. She would make delicious dinners, yummy lunches, and restorative homemade matzo ball soup.

During high school, my mom had bad rheumatoid arthritis and couldn't cook as much as she did when I was younger. So Mom would sit with me in the kitchen, walking me through how to make the meal, helping me out, and giving me instructions as needed. I became a pretty decent cook. I could follow a recipe, and I loved to take a recipe and make it my own.

As I perfected my domestic household skills, I was aware of the fact that I might become a mother myself. But honestly, I didn't think about that option much. I was more career-oriented and artistic-based. Most of my thoughts were consumed with my future career plans and my artistic hobbies: art, writing, design, and drawing. That was more important to me than having a child. Yet I knew that time was coming up eventually in my future.

Throughout my growing-up years, I never thought of myself as anything other than a Jewish female. Although these concepts were never discussed directly, we absorbed the family values of our Jewish community. We knew we were supposed to grow up and follow the "success sequence" that everyone else seemed to follow. First, we would finish school, then we would get married and land a job, then finally, we would have a baby.

No one ever discussed what would happen if these reasonable ideals were derailed. Conversations about being single and pregnant were only spoken in whispers.

"Did you hear that (so and so) was pregnant?"

"What a shame for her family…"

Somewhere along the line, I do remember hearing about women being sent away to have their children and coming back without a child, or being sent to an aunt and uncle's house. How embarrassing it was for the family. There were even times when I remember somebody sitting Shiva because their daughter got pregnant, not with a Jewish person. And that was it.

Sexuality, unplanned pregnancy, and parenthood were absolutely not talked about in my community. They were not discussed in my house at all. Period. Even my friends didn't talk about these topics. They were too shameful. We knew what the Torah said about marriage, and that was all we needed to know. We knew that divorce, unplanned pregnancy, and sex outside of marriage were too shameful to even mention. If we disobeyed the Torah, we would be a complete embarrassment to our families and communities.

Without a word, we absorbed the Jewish community's unspoken feelings about children, abortion, and adoption. Within the orthodox community, abortion was okay. The question boiled down to what was best for the mother: Would the mother be healthy? The decision was all about the mother. If the mother was not going to be healthy through the pregnancy, an abortion would be permitted, as long as she got permission or a dispensation from a rabbi.

The absence of a real discussion of adoption revealed how people commonly viewed and still view adoption: too stigmatized to even be considered. Too painful. Too shameful.

Adoption was seen as fine within the Jewish community—that is, if you were an adoptive parent. Adoptive families were praised for helping the outcast and taking care of the oppressed, just like we are commanded to do in the Torah. All conversations about adoption centered around the parents who took the child in.

But nobody talked about the birth parent. In our community, a birth mother was looked at like a bad guy who didn't matter, someone who did something wrong. As a teenager, I heard the whispers; "It must be drug-related, an adult scumbag who doesn't want or need kids. Why would they do something like that? Why would they give away their child?"

The words "gave away their child" reminded me of a parent who was out there randomly having kids and giving away kids because she had nothing better to do. It filled me with horror.

In high school, I lived in the shadow of my sisters. Some teachers saw me through the lens of my sisters' accomplishments. Even though there was quite an age difference between us, most of my teachers had taught my sisters, and I was always being compared to them.

At first, I tried to do my best. I prided myself on high productivity and efficiency in my work. If I was given an assignment, I made sure it got done, right away. But since I struggled with a learning disability, I knew that I could never live up to my sisters' reputations.

So instead of trying to outshine them, I did everything in my power to avoid being like them. I skipped classes, didn't turn in assignments, and got bells (detention) because of some other things I had done. I was just miserable.

Halfway through my freshman year of high school, I had had enough. Nothing particularly bad happened that day. In most respects, it was just a normal school day. But on the inside, I just snapped. I could not stand living in the shadows of my sisters one minute longer.

Outside my high school, the stately brick Bell Tower of my school stood serene against the lovely fall foliage and soft blue mountains of my Pennsylvania town.

But inside the school bathroom, despair trickled into my soul. Once again, I swallowed as many pills as I could.

After the initial shock of the medication in my body, I had a second shock: my suicide attempt was unsuccessful. Again, I failed to leave this world. Again, I was told, "see a psychiatrist."

This time, I did start seeing a counselor to talk through my issues. I developed a deep bond with the therapist at my high school. His gentle counsel and wisdom helped me through my struggles. With a lot of academic help and a few good friends, I made it to high school graduation with my parents and family looking on.

My parents always loved me, even when I did not love myself. They always pushed me to do better and be better. With their support and my own hard work, I overcame many obstacles and graduated. My hard work and efficiency paid off.

I had no idea how life was about to unravel. And I had no idea how deeply I would fall into despair when I no longer could access my parents' loving support in my life. And when I encountered complex situations that no amount of hard work could do anything to fix.

Chapter 4

A couple of months after I graduated from high school at Wyoming Seminary Upper School in Kingston, Pennsylvania, I was accepted into the Fashion Institute of Technology in New York City. I was told by the college guidance counselor that I would not get into any of the colleges I applied to… but I was accepted into all five. I chose the Fashion Institute.

I had always loved fashion and art. As a child, I would create clothing for my dolls with scarves, do their makeup, and come up with stories behind all of the looks. As I got older, I would often sit with my mother and watch her sew beautiful clothing. Then I would sew on my own. This hobby led me to the Fashion Institute.

The Institute was a tall, artistic, modern building on a street corner. Inside, it was crammed with opportunity. The school contained theaters, workshops, classrooms, and galleries. Students learned about design, fashion, art, exhibition, and television marketing.

I didn't do spectacularly in school because of my learning disability. But despite my difficulty with reading, I somehow managed to finish my way through school for two years.

At first, I worked as a lifeguard in a very posh, upper west side apartment building. I enjoyed meeting the famous people there, and I had a really good time. Soon, I started working full-time as an administrative assistant for an auto advertising firm. I worked for Shriber & Associates for about two years and then moved jobs to Azrak-Hamway, Child Guidance. When my boss moved to Florida, he invited me to transfer there.

"You worked for me in New York," he said. "Would you like to work for me in Florida?"

"No, I like it in New York," I replied.

New York is where I always wanted to be. My parents were originally from Brooklyn. So going to the city was a natural step for me.

I had another reason I wanted to stay in New York: I had just fallen in love. Rick and I had started our life together, and to all appearances, we were happy. I went straight from my college dorm room on 27th street to my boyfriend's apartment in Queens.

Over the next four years, my relationship with Rick was happy. We had our arguments, but we always seemed to be able to work things out. Our relationship was moving forward, and I dreamed of getting married or at least being together for life. Little did I know that our happiness was just my own dream—an illusion.

I think I saw signs that our relationship was not all it was cracked up to be. But I just wasn't ready to deal with them.

One day, I noticed that Rick was not getting ready for work.

"Aren't you going to work today?" I asked him.

"Nah, I've taken the day off," he said.

I frowned slightly into the mirror and continued to do my makeup. As I left the bathroom and bustled around the kitchen preparing my lunch, I saw two movie tickets sitting on the table.

"What are these tickets for?" I asked, suspicion forming in the corners of my mind.

Rick shrugged and chuckled. "Oh, they just gave me two."

I hurried off to work, shrugging off the incident. It wasn't until later that I realized what was going on. I'm pretty sure my boyfriend later took me to visit the person he was seeing. Since she was married, it didn't occur to me that she was likely Rick's mistress.

My mind started to play tricks on me a lot. In the moment, I didn't realize that Rick was manipulative and emotionally abusive. He was never physically harsh, so my mind didn't raise any red flags. But over the years, I've realized what was really going on.

Looking back, we were not as happy as I thought we were. But my euphoric first love told me that our relationship would last. I was still immersed in a fiction of happiness that I had created, so I was not ready for what happened during a trip to my home state.

That fall, my dad was having minor surgery on his hand, so I went back to Pennsylvania to see my parents. I always enjoyed visiting my home and spending time with my family.

One afternoon, my parents and I went out to lunch in the town, enjoying the crisp autumn air and the lovely signs of fall in Pennsylvania. When we returned home, the answering machine was beeping. My dad absentmindedly poked the button to listen to the recording.

"Hello, this is Rick," the voice began.

I wondered what was wrong. Was Rick all right?

"I want to let you know that I'm breaking up with you. You're no longer welcome in my apartment. Bye."

My jaw fell open. I ran to my room and threw myself down on the purple shag carpet. I sobbed uncontrollably for the rest of the afternoon. I was a mess.

I just went home for a few days to be with my family! I screamed silently into my pillow. *And all of a sudden, he breaks up with me! I have nowhere to go back to!*

I had been living with Rick in an apartment in New York, and we were both on the lease. But he made it clear that he wasn't leaving New York. And because I had left, he jumped on the opportunity to kick me out.

I had a job in New York, but they were laying people off, and I knew I was going to be one of the ones that were going to be laid off. I couldn't go back to New York City. I had nothing there. I had nowhere to go.

For days after I got that message, I was in shock.

"What should I do?" I asked my parents. "Where should I go?"

"Go get your stuff and come back home. We'll figure it out," they said.

So I went back to New York City, got my stuff, and came back home. I wasn't in the best mental state to begin with, but from that point on, things got even worse. The whole experience really messed with my head.

My dreams had turned to ashes. My life in New York City, my apartment, my boyfriend, the dreams I had of marriage and children—all of them were gone. Forever. Just like Mom and Dad's wedding photos. All of it had gone up in smoke.

Having nothing to do and nowhere to go, I went to the Woodland Inn and Resort in Wilkes-Barre. I was familiar with the establishment because I had worked there in the past. The hotel was pretty much the only place to hang out in our small town. It had restaurants, shows, musicians, and a swimming pool.

At the inn, I met someone very, very quickly. I didn't really date. Instead, I started sleeping around, drinking, and partying. I was doing things I shouldn't have been doing. I was lost. It was a dark time for me.

The drinks helped to numb everything. Often, I wouldn't come home at night. My parents rarely knew where I was. My dad had a cell phone, which was unusual for the 1990s. He carried it with him everywhere, hoping I would call. But I never did. I came home in the wee hours of the morning, hung over and hopeless.

In November of 1995, I barely noticed I was vomiting more than ever. At first, I thought it was just an excessively big hangover. But then I realized that there was something else going on.

I stood in the bathroom staring at the home pregnancy test. The ten minutes that I waited for the result were the longest ten of my life.

For those long moments, fear and shame flashed through my mind. Getting pregnant was not what any parent wanted for their daughter. Without a doubt, I knew my parents would be deeply disappointed in me if I was pregnant. It would be so deeply shameful. I would be so embarrassed.

These possibilities were absolutely unacceptable to me. They were so terrible that I could not face them.

So it can't be true, I told myself. *It isn't true. I am not pregnant.*

But when I finally saw that the result was positive, my hands flew to my face in terror.

No. This can't be real.

For a while, I stared at the results on the pregnancy test. *My mind has to be playing tricks on me,* I thought. But the longer I stared, the more sickening the terrible reality became. Finally, I went to my room and lay on my bed. I didn't have anyone to talk to. I didn't have a clue what to do.

So I got up and went to the Woodlands and partied more with my friends. If I could live as if it *wasn't* real, maybe it would all just go away. I was in deep denial.

After three months, I knew I had to face what was going on. I finally allowed myself to think about my predicament for more than a fleeting moment. As I admitted to myself this terrible reality, I began to sink deeply. Shame, anger, and terror filled me.

I am twenty-three and single. I don't know who the father is.

I knew that I had failed to follow the "success sequence" that everyone else seemed to follow. I knew it well: "First you finish school, then you get married and land a job, then you have a baby." Of course, this was a very reasonable goal. But I knew my Jewish community would ignore or punish harshly those who broke the sequence.

I was deeply broken, like that radio my dad had tried to fix. Like him, I was great at taking my life apart. I could tell you something was wrong and that something wasn't working. But I had no idea how to fix it.

I was lost, like the Afikomen my parents had hidden when I was little. Yet no one was coming to find me. I was broken, and no one was healing me. I was enslaved to my passions and mistakes, like the Israelites in Egypt, and it seemed like no one was going to deliver me. I had to deal with it myself.

I'd always prided myself on hard work, productivity, and efficiency. But I'd encountered a situation that was far beyond me. If only motherhood could be as simple as checking off the boxes.

I turned the options over in my mind. I tried to reason.

I can take care of myself economically, but not emotionally. I can't imagine taking care of a baby 24/7. I can't even seem to take care of myself! I am not ready to raise a baby. It wouldn't be good for either of us.

I needed to do something. I was pregnant, single, alone, and ashamed. I couldn't deal with it, and I didn't want to deal with it.

Having a baby was uncharted territory. There were no checklists, no maps, and no script. But there was a way I could take action.

Abortion… maybe that would be a good option.

At this point, I felt it was my only option.

Chapter 5

Three and a half weeks after I found out I was pregnant, I called my friend and told him my choice.

"Can you come drive me to the abortion clinic?" I asked.

"Isn't it too late to have an abortion?" he asked. "You're already at 13-14 weeks. Isn't that the cutoff?"

"I don't know," I said, "but I have to find out. I can't keep this baby."

"Okay, I'll come pick you up tomorrow," he agreed.

The next day, he drove over an hour to take me to the clinic. As we were driving, I didn't say a word. I was scared and confused. I just didn't know what to think or where to turn.

He didn't say much either. I found out later he didn't really support the idea of having an abortion, but he was there for me anyway.

We pulled into the clinic's parking lot in Hazelton, Pennsylvania. It was a simple white building with a blue stripe near the top. I walked through the chilly November air, my head bowed against the stiff, biting wind.

Inside the warm waiting room, as I waited for the nurse, thoughts swirled in my mind.

Getting an abortion will erase all the shame... the shame from conceiving a baby with a complete stranger... the shame of being unable, right now, to raise the baby I conceived... the shame that will come from my family finding out.

Most of all, I wanted to avoid the shame of potentially being labeled "a bad mother" who "gave away" her child for adoption. In my Jewish community, placing a child for adoption came with a high stigma.

A nurse came out and started speaking to me, but I couldn't hear or understand a word she was saying. I just heard her say, "Fill this out."

I started filling out the pre-abortion paperwork, writing in the details.

"I am due mid-April... my birthdate is..."

But before I could even finish the questionnaire or enter the clinic examination room, my tears began to wash over the clipboard on my lap.

Although I wanted to erase my shame, I knew I could not bear to do it at the expense of the tiny baby growing inside me. I was and always have been pro-choice. However, being pro-choice did not equal wanting to abort. I realized this as I was sitting at the clinic, tears continuing to fall on the paper in my hand.

This is not for me. I can't do this.

I threw my pen down in mid-word.

"Let's go," I told my friend. We bolted.

I walked out of the clinic, not knowing what I would do next but knowing that I could not terminate my pregnancy, no matter how hard it was.

We climbed into the car without a word and retraced our path back home. My friend's silent, supportive presence was a comfort, but it couldn't begin to touch the confusion and pain in my heart.

All I could think of as I drove home was, *How did I get here?*

Of course, from my outward circumstances, it made sense why I had just visited an abortion clinic. I was alone, ashamed, and afraid.

But from my adult perspective, the situation was much more complex. If I could, I would put my arm around my younger self and say, "Why are you here? That's a very good question."

In the Hebrew language, the word for "compassion" is derived from the word "womb." It makes sense that the deepest feeling of compassion in the world is that of a mother for her child. Yet many Jewish women feel pressured to abort as their first and only resort.

The question, "Why am I here," is more complex than it looks at first glance. What factors contributed to the journey I was on?

Why did I start my journey at an abortion clinic instead of an adoption agency?

Why is placing a baby for adoption so rare in the Jewish community?

Why was adoption my last resort—when clearly, in my heart, something was telling me not to abort and parenting was not an option?

I am pro-choice, and I believe a woman should truly have a choice about what happens to her life and the life of her unborn child. Yet because of the shame and stigma, many Jewish women don't truly have a choice. They see abortion as their only option.

That November day, I didn't have a voice or a choice. I had no way to know that one day, I would become a courageous and outspoken speaker and writer, advocating for Jewish women to truly have a choice. But that hope-filled future was veiled by a mist of fear.

As I drove home that gray November afternoon, I could only think about the tiny life whose heart was still beating inside of me. I could only think of my still-bleak future, without a home, a job, or a life partner.

I had no idea what I was going to do next.

When I got home, my mind kicked into high gear. There was absolutely no way that I was going to stay in Pennsylvania. My pregnancy was a shame to myself, but it would also be a shame to my entire family if anyone found out.

I absolutely cannot let my parents know about this, I thought. *I have to get out as fast as I can.*

Suddenly thinking clearly, I remembered the boss who had asked me to work for him in Florida.

"You know, I'm going to reach out to him," I thought.

Within a few days, the man had responded.

"Of course we would like to have you work for us!" he said. "You have the job. When can you be here?"

Everyone was happy for me. They assumed I left the state for a new and successful job, which technically was true. But no one knew the secret I held inside of me.

Within a week, I packed my bags and moved for a job more than 1,000 miles away. As I drove away, I felt a deep sense of relief. I could not bear the thought of my family discovering I was pregnant. I could not bear seeing their reaction to me. I did not want to see them label me as what I already knew I was.

An embarrassment.

The warm, humid air of Florida was very different from the crisp weather in Pennsylvania. Colorful, low-lying homes replaced the rustic, colonial architecture back east. I was suddenly surrounded by palm trees instead of sugar maples.

When I first moved to Florida, I settled down in Boca Raton and worked at a toy manufacturer as an Administrative Assistant. I found an apartment. I still didn't really know what I was doing, but I was finding my way.

"Okay, I have a job. At least I have a job," I said to myself. "That's a huge start."

Every day, the toys reminded me of the child I was carrying. The baby was growing bigger and bigger, and I didn't know what to do next. I realized I needed to figure out what to do about this pregnancy.

I was already about four months pregnant. It was getting to the point that I really needed to make a decision. If I was going to have an abortion, I would need to do it pretty much immediately. I needed to figure out what my next step was going to be.

Do I keep the baby? Do I place her for adoption? How does one make that decision, especially alone?

I did not have anyone to talk to. I had no one to bounce my ideas off. No family, no friends, no rabbis.

I thought about trying an abortion again. I thought about the trauma it causes the body. The idea that people use abortion as birth control is so misguided. Why would someone want to put her body through that? That's a hard decision. I thought long and hard about my options. Finally, I made my choice.

"Okay, I'll try to go for an abortion again."

When I called the abortion clinic, the receptionist had bad news for me.

"Sorry, honey, you're already past twenty-four weeks. We don't do abortions past twenty-four weeks," the honey-voiced lady told me.

I hung up the phone and hung my head in fear and shame. But there was no time to waste. If I couldn't abort the baby, I really did need to find another option—and quickly.

I still knew I could take care of myself economically, but not emotionally. I could pay my own way. But to have another soul I was responsible for around the clock? A living being depending on me for her every need? I couldn't do it. I still knew I was not ready to raise a baby.

The baby will grow up to be a whole new human being... I can't be responsible for that. I don't know how to raise a responsible human.

The only option left was adoption.

Chapter 6

Once I'd made my decision, I started to search. The Internet was not what it is now, and I didn't know anyone who had a computer. I could go to the library to use a computer, but it wasn't accessible. Google didn't exist, and I couldn't figure out where to start.

How do you pick an adoption attorney? I had no idea. So I literally picked up the yellow pages. I flipped open the book, smelling the fresh scent of newsprint. I found the page for adoption attorneys, closed my eyes, and pointed. My finger was near a giant, colorful ad.

Perfect. How about this one?

It's not like I could ask anyone. I wasn't a paralegal and couldn't figure out the whole legal system. I couldn't call and see if the attorney had any strikes against her. I couldn't read reviews. So I chose the one with the biggest and brightest ad and hoped for the best.

I made the call, and she set up the appointment. Scared and embarrassed, I walked into her office and sat down. I must have had a blank look on my face.

"Okay, what do I do?" I asked.

I didn't know what questions to ask, so I just did as I was told.

The attorney sat me down and said, "Before we even move forward, we need you to go to Doctor A, Doctor B, this office, that office."

I went through the questionnaire the attorney gave me, then headed to the OBGYN for the tests. After running around for several days, taking all the tests, I found out I had passed.

"Your next step is to choose your adoptive parents," the attorney informed me, handing me a thick notebook. On her shelf, the attorney had notebook after notebook after notebook. They were full of biographies of families who wanted to become parents through adoption. She was still holding one in my direction.

I took one of the notebooks and sat down. I had no idea what I was doing. The only thing I knew was that I wanted an open adoption. Although an open adoption means different things to different people, open adoption means you have some sort of communication with the adoptive family. This was first and foremost for me. I wanted to hear from my baby: find out how he or she was doing, receive monthly updates, and get pictures.

I especially looked forward to getting the pictures. Ever since the fire when I was in eighth grade, photographs had become treasures. Family connections were so precious to me. After all, this baby was my son or daughter. If I couldn't spend every minute with my baby, watching him or her grow up, I at least wanted to get pictures. In an open adoption, I would be able to watch the baby grow up and at least know he or she was safe, healthy, and happy.

I opened the notebook. Each page contained a picture and a paragraph, three to four lines about each family. From this scant information, I was supposed to make a decision that would affect my child's life forever.

Sitting there with looseleaf notebooks full of pictures and a paragraph about why the families wanted to adopt, I suddenly felt overwhelmed. I had just been assigned the task of picking the family who would raise my child. The job in front of me was ironic, surreal, and daunting.

Because I hadn't been making the best decisions when I got pregnant, I didn't have a whole lot of things on my checklist that were a must. How was I supposed to know what kind of parents should raise my child? I had just two requirements on my list. The family had to be well-established. And Jewish.

It seemed like picking a Jewish family would help me stay connected to my baby. On every holiday or feast day, I could think about my child, celebrating the same special event with his or her adoptive parents. It would be a way to connect with him or her.

After hours of carefully studying adoption albums, I had narrowed down my search to two families. From the photo and brief synopsis, the first family seemed to fulfill my requirements: well-established and Jewish. They also seemed secure, loving, and responsible. But the other family seemed like a good option, as well. It was a tough decision, but I finally decided on the first family.

A few days later, I got the scoop from the attorney.

"I called the family and spoke with them, and the adoptive family has agreed to meet with you. Are you willing to meet the family tomorrow?"

"Sure," I said.

But as the meeting got closer, the hours stretched into some of the longest in my life.

What in the world have I gotten myself into? I wondered. *Will this family really be able to give my baby all that she will need emotionally? If she's anything like me, they'll have their hands full.*

The weight of my decision pounded down on me, a heavy pressure in my chest. I knew I could still back out if I wanted to. But I'd already backed out of the abortion. If I didn't follow through with this opportunity, I may not have a second chance.

As I walked into the attorney's office the next day, my heart was pounding so hard it almost hurt. I reached my hand out and politely shook hands with both the husband and the wife.

"Hi, great to meet you," said the adoptive mother. Her long, nervous face was hidden in a crown of curls.

"It's a pleasure," said the dad, his merry eyes smiling out of his jolly round face.

"I'm Lori," I murmured. My palms were sweaty.

I sat down on one of the faded turquoise chairs, but I still couldn't get my heart to calm down. I was sure that the couple felt just as awkward as I did. And they were surely judging me. They were Jewish, after all.

My brain was everywhere.

I am literally picking the family that my baby will be with for the rest of her life.

The fears overwhelmed me. My head started to swim, and I felt dizzy. At the time, I had no way to know what I was feeling. I was not familiar with the symptoms of a panic attack or anxiety attack. And I had no idea that this was just the beginning of an ever-intensifying journey with fear.

I hoped the meeting would be over as soon as possible. The family was judging me, and to be honest, I was judging them, too. I had to make a monumental choice: selecting a family for my child. I wanted to make sure they were worthy of my trust.

This is so awkward.

The attorney was staring at all three of us, asking perfunctory questions and not looking like she was enjoying the meeting very much. Now, looking back, I think she was likely just worrying about the $20,000 to $30,000 she would get out of all of us if the meeting was a success.

After a very stilted ten-minute conversation, the conversation was winding down.

"What do you think, Lori?" the attorney asked the pointed question. "Do you want to choose this couple to parent your baby?"

Despite my reservations, I squeaked out the words, "Yes, these are the ones."

We shook hands and I fled out of the office as quickly as I could.

Neither the attorney nor the couple told me at the time that the adoptive family had actually been searching for a Jewish birth mother, just like I was searching for a Jewish adoptive family. Finding a Jewish birth mother was one of their "musts," a non-negotiable. This was a very unusual request in our cultural milieu, since Jewish people didn't often place their children for adoption, or at least didn't talk about it. Perhaps this was meant to be.

When I learned about their request years later, it helped me feel more peaceful about my decision. If I had known this little tidbit of information when I first met the couple, perhaps I would have felt calmer and more settled as I navigated the rough and uncomfortable waters that lay ahead in my relationship with the adoptive family.

Over the next few months, the adoptive family and I met several times. We went out for dinner together, and they took me to South Beach. As we explored the bright lights and attractions of the beach town, I felt for a moment like I was in paradise. The palm trees waved gently above the outdoor patio table we sat at. In that brief instant in time, I closed my eyes and let the warm sunshine soak into my face. The sounds of children playing, tourists gawking, and shorebirds squabbling held me in a trance.

But only seconds later, the voice of the adoptive mother cut into my reverie.

"Can you give us a bit more information about your health background?" she wondered, getting out a pen and notepad. "Do you have a history of cancer, heart attacks, or other disorders in your family? How about mental health? We want to be able to give the baby accurate information about his or her health history."

It was true. They had a valid point, and I knew I needed to be honest with them. Since they were going to raise my child, they needed to know these things.

But I still felt so self-conscious and weird. Our conversations never moved past surface stuff. The whole relationship seemed surreal and extremely awkward and stilted.

The couple never even told me their last name. The attorney wasn't forthcoming about the adoptive family's identifying information, and I didn't think to ask. The attorney had told me it was part of the legal process to keep the adoptive parents partially anonymous. How was I supposed to know that the attorney wasn't always following the legal regulations of our state? I didn't know what was going to happen, and I had no experience with adoption or the legal system.

Does this couple really care about me as a person? I would sometimes wonder. *Or do they only care about the child I am going to provide for them?*

Deep down, I wished someone would care about my feelings, my fears, and my future—not just the baby's. I wished someone would fill the parental role that my parents would not fill. But the surface-level questions the adoptive parents asked indicated they would never fill that role for me.

I took a deep breath and started listing every health condition I knew about in my extended family. Then our chatter fell silent again. I listened to the sound of the gulls.

As spring approached, I began to relax. Everything was going okay. I was able to continue working all the way through my pregnancy, and I'd succeeded in hiding my pregnancy from my boss and coworkers. Every morning, I pulled on a loose, gauzy A-line dress and breezed into the job, with no one the wiser. It was Florida, and it was okay to wear loose dresses.

No one knew about my pregnancy. This would make it easier when the time came to give birth. No one would ask me what had happened to the baby. I would be able to go on as if nothing had happened.

I was also feeling more confident about my relationship with the adoptive parents. Though we had never exchanged contact information, we'd attempted to get to know one another. I noticed I was feeling a bit more comfortable and relaxed when we spent time together.

Sitting in a fancy restaurant near South Beach, the family and I discussed the baby's name.

"We've decided to honor your name choice by keeping the names you choose, one or both of them," the dad smiled.

I breathed deeply, letting the tension out.

"Thank you," I said. "I'm looking forward to keeping in touch after the baby's birth, getting the photos and updates about how the baby's life is progressing."

"We'll certainly send them," the adoptive mom promised.

I took a sip of ice water.

Maybe I made the right decision after all.

Then the day from hell came. I was watching Oprah on TV. What else? It was the 90s. I was watching a show about a bunch of comedians: "What your mother didn't tell you about being pregnant." It was supposed to be funny, comical, and light.

It did not hit me in that way. Instead, as I watched the show, I became increasingly anxious. My throat was constricting. My heart was pounding. My chest throbbed. Everything was going black. My stomach hurt.

What is going on? Is everything okay?

I clasped my chest, my mouth dry. I was starting to tremble. I could feel my heart in my chest, first throbbing, then skipping, then pulsing extra hard. Fear shot through me like an arrow.

I am having a heart attack. I think I am dying. If I don't do something, the baby is going to die.

Nobody spoke about anxiety in those ways in the late 1990s. You didn't hear about anxiety on the television or radio. So I didn't know what was wrong with me. And on top of all that, I was pregnant. Hormones and fear washed over me.

I didn't have anyone I could call. I was alone in my apartment. Although I had a job, I was alone the rest of the time. I was so embarrassed about my pregnancy that I didn't associate with my family. I didn't have any friends, and I didn't know who the father was. Who could help me?

Suddenly, I had an idea.

I could call my baby's adoptive mother! Surely, she would support me! She said to call her anytime.

Quickly, I reached for the phone receiver and dialed the adoptive mom's pager number. A few minutes later, she called me back. I eagerly grabbed the phone and held it to my ear.

"I don't have time to deal with you right now," came the harsh reply.

I slammed the receiver back into its plastic cradle, panicked tears springing spontaneously to my eyes. I sobbed, hugged myself, and rocked back and forth.

I think I'm dying! The baby might be in danger! And she doesn't have time for me? Then how is she going to have time for my child? Because if my baby's going to be anything like me, it's not going to be an easy road.

I sniffed into a tissue and rumpled the pages of the notebook until I found the page where the attorney's number was written. It was the same page where I'd scrawled it excitedly the first day I found her ad in the Yellow Pages.

Now, I only had one option. I picked up the phone again.

"I am not giving my child to this family," I stated bluntly as the attorney picked up the line.

She tried to convince and manipulate and cajole, but my mind was made up.

"I'm not doing it," I told her, and hung up.

Twenty minutes after the phone call, I heard a knock at my door.

Odd… I don't have any friends.

I timidly looked through the peephole and saw my attorney's paralegal on my porch. She just showed up, out of the blue.

"Pack your bag," she said bluntly when I opened the door a crack. "You're coming to my house for the weekend."

Chapter 7

That weekend was lovely. The paralegal's family was very wealthy. We spent the weekend shopping. The hectic noise of the mall, the neon lights above the shops, and the excitement of picking new clothes kept my mind in a whirl. We went to movies, filled our stomachs with popcorn, and practically hung out in paradise. The entire weekend, the paralegal's family kept me busy. There was no downtime except for sleep. No time to plan, think, get out of this, or realize I was outnumbered by the attorney and her crew.

I had no way to recognize this as a tactic of psychological manipulation. The paralegal and the attorney worked hard to keep me busy, keep me from thinking, and distract me from my pain and discouragement. I know now that the attorney and her paralegal wanted to cheer me up, calm me down, and get me back to the place where I needed to be in order to give the baby up for adoption—so I would give the attorney her money.

It worked. When I went back to my apartment Sunday night so I could get ready for work on Monday morning, I felt better.

"It will be fine," I said to myself. The mom had apologized, and I held onto that. I had enjoyed the weekend with the paralegal. It seemed obvious that the attorney and the paralegal cared about me. They were the only friends I had, and I wanted the friendship to continue.

"Yes, we can move ahead with the plans," I told the attorney.

That was the beginning of the end. I closed my heart, put everything behind me, and compartmentalized. I put it away, didn't deal with it, didn't want to deal with it.

Whenever I had another panic attack, I didn't tell anyone. I didn't want someone to show up at my apartment again. It was great to get out of my apartment, but looking back, I hated it. To what end were they spending time with me? And how was I supposed to recognize the ulterior motives? I didn't know what to do.

As the baby's birth approached, I settled on a name. If I had a girl, I wanted to name her Olivia Anastasia: Olivia after Olivia de Haviland, a favorite actress of mine, and Anastasia after the character she played in Anastasia: The Mystery of Anna.

About six weeks before my baby's due date, the paralegal urged me to practically move in with her. I spent a lot of time with her. I enjoyed the feeling of having someone looking after me, and her rich home was a lot more interesting than my apartment.

I didn't realize just how important it was to the attorney and paralegal to make sure they supported me and kept their eyes on me through that difficult, hormonal transition into motherhood. They wanted to make sure I didn't change my mind.

I didn't realize until many years later what was actually happening. I just thought I was being looked after. But in reality, my situation was a bit like legal human trafficking. The attorney and the paralegal were just trying to get money. But I was alone and pregnant, and there was no way I could realize that.

One day, I noticed that the pain in my abdomen strongly resembled the contractions I'd heard about on that traumatizing Oprah show. It was the afternoon of March 22, 1996, and I was at the paralegal's house.

"I don't know what's going on," I said to the paralegal.

"Honey, I think you're going into labor," the paralegal said.

"But I'm not even 35 weeks," I protested.

"I've been around tons of pregnant women, and I'm pretty sure that's what's going on," the paralegal said. "We'd better get you to the hospital."

"I don't want to go to the hospital until I absolutely have to," I said.

That afternoon, the contractions intensified. Finally, around 6:00 p.m., I gave in.

"Let's go," I said to the paralegal.

The paralegal checked me into the hospital, while the attorney's tall associate looked on. Then we walked upstairs to the birthing wing.

As I labored, I missed my mother. She had been at my side for so many huge life events. She had always tried to support me during the worst moments in my story. She had sat by my side and listened to me cry when I was a suicidal teen. And if I had reached out to her during this pregnancy, I'm sure she would have worked hard to make sure I was healthy and that the baby was healthy.

But at the time, I wasn't one hundred percent sure she would be supportive. And because of my own choices, I was alone. It was so hard to do this without my mother's support. As waves of pain washed over me, I did the only thing I knew to do: kept pressing forward.

Soon it will all be over and I can move on with life, I comforted myself between contractions.

Seven hours later, on March 23, 1996, my baby girl was born. She was tiny, only a little over four pounds, but otherwise, she was perfectly healthy.

"Since she was born six weeks early, we need to take her to the NICU and check her out," the nurse told me.

"Do you think she'll be okay?" I said with concern.

"Yes, she looks perfectly healthy," said the doctor. "But to be on the safe side, we need to put her in the NICU, just to make sure everything is fine. But I'll let you hold her first and say goodbye."

As the nurse placed her in my arms, I felt her warm weight against my chest. I stared.

I just gave birth to my first daughter.

She had a tiny bit of peach fuzz that crowned her bright red face. When she raised her eyebrows, her entire forehead wrinkled. Her tiny cheeks were covered in the softest, finest hairs. She had long fingers and the most minuscule fingernails I had ever seen. She was inexpressibly adorable.

Pain rushed through my heart like an unstoppable flood. The nurse was standing nearby, waiting to take my baby to the NICU. To rip her away from me forever.

How can I do this? How can I hand her to the nurse? How can I say goodbye and never see her again? She'll never realize that I love her with my entire heart.

I started to sob uncontrollably.

"Olivia," I choked out. "I am so sorry."

I took her tiny hand in mine. Her gray-blue eyes considered me silently.

"I know it's hard for you to understand, but I chose adoption because I wanted you to have a happy life where

71

you would have two responsible parents," I sobbed. The past few months flashed through my mind. All the heartache. All the awkwardness. All the doubts and fears. But I pressed on. "I knew I couldn't take good care of you. I chose people who are stable and established. They will take good care of you. I want what is best for you."

I couldn't go on. I was crying hysterically. The whole gamut of things was going through my brain. The nurse was waiting.

"I love you so, so much. I will think about you every day of my life. I will never forget you, Olivia."

The nurse reached down and lifted the lightweight, frail, bundle out of my arms.

The nurse settled her in her arms. "Off to the NICU we go," she was crooning to Olivia as she walked out the door.

Sobs burst out of me, as powerful as a freight train.

I will never see my daughter again.

The legal team was packing their bags and walking out with the nurse. I was completely alone.

The adoptive family had taken a vacation, their last vacation with just the two of them. Since I went into labor six weeks early, they were still away from home.

My parents and sisters still didn't know. I felt like I was holding the hugest secret. How could I have done this—bringing a new life into the world without the knowledge and support of my mother and family? Mom had always been there for me, comforting me in the darkest times. But now, I was alone. And I wasn't sure that she would be here for me, even if she did know. That would be the hugest rejection imaginable—one I didn't want to face the reality of.

After the birth, the nurse started wheeling me out of the labor and delivery room to another recovery room on the same floor with the babies.

"Please, please give me a room on another floor," I begged.

The nurse paused, concern and puzzlement written all over her face. "We always keep moms on the same floor as the babies," she said.

"Please help me find a room somewhere else," I pleaded.

I loved babies; I'd always been a baby person. But I couldn't stand to hear the cries, the hiccups, and the snuffles of the infants with their mothers. I couldn't bear to hear the happy, supportive laughter of friends and families coming to see their newborn relatives.

"Okay," the nurse finally agreed, wheeling me to another floor and settling me into the bed.

I left the hospital the next day. Before I left, I asked how the baby was doing.

"She's 100% fine," the nurse said. "She'll be released from the NICU today or tomorrow morning. She's great!"

The nurse smiled compassionately. Then she sent me on my way. I went back to the paralegal's house to get my stuff.

"Do you want to go ahead and sign away your parental rights today, so you don't have to come back later?" the paralegal suggested.

"No, I'll do it in a couple of days," I said.

On the inside, I was shouting, *I'm not signing anything today!* I knew there was a three-day period where I could rescind my legal rights. There was a waiting period in which I could still change my mind. If anything came up during that time, I didn't want to act rashly.

I went back to my apartment and cried nonstop for the rest of the evening. My arms ached for the baby. My heart literally hurt. I just wanted to hold Olivia in my arms. To plant one more kiss on her forehead. To feed her and make sure she was all right.

Questions swarmed through my mind.

What have I done?

How could I have done this?

Does Olivia miss me like I miss her?

I felt physically sick. Adjusting to being home postpartum is tough even if you're going home with the baby. Much more if you're not! I couldn't stop the questions.

Did I make the right choice?

Is the family back from their vacation?

Are they taking good care of Olivia?

The questions swirled, but there were no answers. That night, I cried myself to sleep.

I woke up the next morning with a deep emptiness. Moments went by slowly, like molasses. I felt like I had cried all the tears in the world. But after a few hours, I burst into uncontrollable sobs again.

I knew that if I just spoke the word, I could have my baby back. But I'd already changed my mind enough times on this journey. I had walked out of the abortion office. I couldn't walk out of my adoption option, too. I had no baby supplies and was not prepared to parent.

Three days after Olivia was born, the dreaded moment arrived. I had to go to the attorney's office to relinquish my parental rights. Before I left for the attorney's office, I painstakingly wrote a letter to my daughter.

"I love you, and I always will," I finished the letter through eyes blurry with tears.

Then I headed to the attorney's office.

Before I signed the relinquishment papers, I gave the attorney the letter I had written to my daughter. I wanted to ensure the adoptive parents received it.

"Please make sure this letter gets to my daughter," I said.

I took a deep breath and bravely signed my name on the dotted line. As a parting gift, the attorney gave me a legal piece of paper. The paralegal beamed. She was all smiles now. I didn't realize just exactly what was at stake for her, or just how much money changed hands with every adoption. They basically bought my child. In a private adoption, tens of thousands of dollars are paid to the attorney in exchange for a child. It's basically human trafficking.

As a part of the process, the attorney had paid some of my medical expenses and bills because I couldn't afford them. She gave me my last check after I signed the paperwork.

Then I left the attorney's office, alone.

A few days later, I lay in a hospital bed again, moaning in pain and loneliness. I had come down with an infection that landed me back in the very same hospital where I had recently said goodbye to Olivia. Every sight, sound, and smell in the hospital brought back heartbreaking memories of my separation from Olivia. The memories were still so raw and traumatic. As I lay in bed, alone, pain radiated through my body. Fear radiated through my heart. My tears started to flow, like a faucet I could not turn off.

Now that I had officially signed away my parental rights, there was no more attorney and no more support at all from anyone in the office. Their kind, benevolent gestures stopped the moment I signed my name on the dotted line. The paralegal and the attorney took the money from the adoptive parents, delivered the paperwork that assured the adoptive parents' legal rights, and practically disappeared without a trace. They were done with me. They offered no help, no one to check up on me, and no aftercare physically or emotionally. Grief is normal after an adoption, but I did not have anyone to support me. Because no one helped me process those traumatic memories, some of them are still with me today.

I spent two weeks in the hospital, crying. Then the doctors sent me home. I arrived in my apartment, saddled with all the problems I had had before Olivia was conceived—plus the life-changing grief of losing her to adoption. I was alone, and I had no idea where to turn.

My only consolation was that soon, I would receive an update on how my baby was doing.

Chapter 8

Day after day, I waited for the first update from Olivia's new family. I checked my answering machine frequently to see if the adoptive family had called. I was eager to hear an update about my baby.

My mind was filled with questions. *Were the nurses correct when they said that Olivia was perfect and 100% okay? Or does my baby have lingering side effects from being born early? Is she growing healthy and strong? Does she still look like my side of the family, or are there more characteristics from the other side of the family that are coming out as she gets older?*

I checked the mailbox every day, hoping against hope that today's mail had brought me news of Olivia. When nothing arrived, I tried to explain it away.

I bet they're busy with the newborn, I reasoned. *They forgot this month. But they'll remember next month. If not, the attorney will remind them. She promised.*

After several months had gone by with no changes, I decided to ask the attorney.

"I haven't gotten any photos yet," I said. "Would you be willing to check on the adoptive parents?"

"Once the adoption went through, you have no rights," the attorney told me, hanging up rapidly.

The attorney wasn't going to lift a finger to help me. I would just have to wait and see. After many more months, I concluded that the parents must have made the decision not to keep me informed or keep in contact. The crushing disappointment of not getting the letter was too much to bear. I sat down and cried a river of tears.

Eventually, I got tired of crying. It was exhausting and depleting. So I stopped crying. Without tears, I was an empty, hollow void. As months went by with no news of Olivia, my mind feared the worst.

Did she die? Is she okay? Have the birth parents forgotten me?

These thoughts were too difficult to allow into my mind, so I stuffed them down. It was nearly impossible to deal with the intensity of the emotions I was feeling, so I shut them off. In the vacuum, the depression intensified, but I tried to move on.

Moving on was not as easy as it seemed. With no advocate, no support, and no one to help me move forward with my life, I quickly went into a downward spiral. Since I had cut ties with my family because of embarrassment, I had no friends or relatives to support me. I was stuck with all the problems I had before, plus the loss.

Lost, desperate, and alone, I looked for love in all the wrong places. Before long, I found a tall and handsome Tanzanian guy named Kito. Just seven months after Olivia's birth, I was pregnant with Kito's child. As soon as I found out I was expecting another baby, my mind was made up.

At least this time I know who the father is, I thought. *I know one thing for sure: I am not going to be one of those women who places two children for adoption. And I'm not going to have an abortion. I am going to raise this baby— on my own if I have to. Somehow, some way, I am going to make this work.*

But then I found out I would not have to raise her alone. Kito wanted to marry me.

"You are pregnant with my baby," Kito said. "We have to get married. Why wouldn't I want to be with you?"

I knew he had another reason as well. He wanted to get married so he could get his green card. He was an immigrant who had come in legally and stayed past his deadline. Now, marrying an American citizen would be a huge benefit to him. Although I saw all the signs and signals of abuse, I still stayed with Kito.

Throughout my relationship with him, I had been biding my time. I knew he didn't treat me great, so I refused to make a commitment. Now that I was pregnant, things were different. I didn't know what else to do, so Kito and I got married.

My pregnancy with Ruby was fairly easy. Besides the undiagnosed postpartum depression and grief from Olivia's birth, I didn't have many health issues. If the pregnancy reminded me of the trauma of my first pregnancy, I did not allow myself to think about it. Whenever I had flashbacks and feelings about Olivia, I compartmentalized them and refused to deal with them. I didn't want to think about that anymore.

I continued working at Centerline Homes as a secretary in Coral Springs, Florida. Every morning, I drove forty-five minutes from Delray Beach. As I drove, I thought about my life. That commute was my time. I unwound. I relaxed. I pondered. After work every afternoon, I was very grateful for that time to decompress from the stresses of the day. I knew that when I got home and saw Kito, I would be walking into hell.

By the time the baby's due date approached, we had moved to Boynton Beach. Our little apartment didn't have a washer or dryer, so I had to lug the heavy bags of clothes ten minutes down the street to the nearest laundromat. With my giant belly and my bulging sacks of laundry, the process was exhausting. I couldn't wait to give birth.

A few days later, the familiar clenching pain was coming on faster and harder. I breathed deeply, trying to keep my composure. Kito was in the bathroom, staring intently into the mirror, shaving his hair.

I'm in labor and all he can think about is his hair, I found myself thinking. At least when I was in labor with Olivia, I'd had a paralegal to support me. Now, I felt more alone than ever.

I heard him muttering to himself as he shaved.

Moments later, I felt the familiar rush of water down my legs. My water had broken.

"Kito, I think it's time to go to the hospital," I said, timidly but urgently.

"I have to finish shaving my head," Kito said absentmindedly.

"But I'm having the baby!" I objected.

He turned and pinned me with his eyes. "Do you think I can go to the hospital looking like this? Only half my head shaved?"

He turned nonchalantly back to the mirror and continued ever so carefully cutting his hair. By the time we finally made it to the hospital, I was contorted with pain.

"Drop me off, please," I begged.

"I need to find a place to park," Kito objected.

"Nope. Drop me off in front," I said, my voice becoming more urgent.

For once, he listened to me. The car dashboard read 12:00 p.m. when I staggered out of the car. Kito casually took his time parking while I checked in at the front desk. I was convulsing with pain as the nurses escorted me to my bed.

"Who will hold the baby first?" a friendly nurse quizzed me after I got settled in the room.

"Her dad is holding her first," I barely managed to gasp in between contractions.

Although I didn't let myself think about the reason I had made this choice, I know now why I wanted Kito to hold her first. Subconsciously, I refused to re-enter that painful moment when I held Olivia in my arms for the first time. Because of the still-fresh loss, I didn't want to be the first one to touch this precious, newborn treasure.

At 12:28 p.m., my second child was born, beautiful, russet, healthy, and screaming. Thankfully, Kito had finally finished parking and had arrived just minutes before his child was born. As planned, Kito took Ruby in his arms, the first to hold her.

The rest of my time in the hospital was a blur. Little Ruby and I were dismissed two days later. When we got home, Kito sat down on the couch to watch TV. He didn't even look up as he delivered his nonchalant message:

"Hey, the laundry needs to be done."

A deep heaviness settled in my chest. The laundromat wasn't far, but I had just given birth. At that moment, all I wanted was to lie down, hold my baby, and rest. But I knew that was not possible.

Still aching and sore from childbirth, feeling like I was oozing from every pore, I gathered together the trash bags full of laundry. I dragged the bags, and my fragile three-day-old baby, to the laundromat ten minutes away. This wasn't any easier than doing laundry with a pregnant belly.

An hour later, as I pulled laundry out of the dryer, some compassionate workers noticed I was in trouble. They could see me grimacing whenever I lifted the laundry baskets.

"Are you okay?" they asked.

"I just gave birth," I replied, as an explanation.

"But why are you out here doing laundry so soon? Here, let me help you with that laundry basket. You just sit down and hold the baby for a minute. Is there anything else you need to share? Do you need help?"

I wanted to tell more, but I knew Kito wouldn't let me. I wasn't allowed to talk to anybody or see anybody. So I just smiled politely and shook my head.

The weeks went by in a blur. Post-partum depression, which had never really left me after Olivia was born, redoubled its vengeful grip on my life. Once or twice, I went to the local Jewish synagogue. Some of the congregation at the local temple were kind to me as well. A gentle rabbi, Rabbi Kaplan, seemed to feel genuine compassion for me. The shul seemed like my only haven from my desperate life.

I was still not talking to my parents. They did not know about Olivia and most certainly did not know that I had gotten married and had Ruby. I had no idea what I was doing, and I felt like I was just digging myself deeper and deeper into a web of secrecy, loneliness, and despair.

"We need to get Ruby baptized," Kito said to me one day.

"But I thought you said we were raising her Jewish!" I said. "We agreed on that! We can't baptize a Jewish baby."

Kito shrugged. With that one shrug, he was saying that all our plans about raising her Jewish were going out the window. I deeply wanted my daughter to be named in my own Jewish synagogue, like I had been when I was born. It was customary for baby girls to be named in a traditional ceremony that corresponded to the circumcision or bris ceremony of Jewish male children.

I have to get her named in the correct Jewish way, I thought desperately. *I can't let Kito's church name her. What can I do?*

My mind immediately came up with an answer: *Call Mom.* Mom hadn't heard from me in about eight months, and she didn't even know Ruby existed. But it was my only option.

I had to walk to a pay phone down the street to make the call. Kito was very sensitive about calls on our house phone; whenever he saw an unfamiliar phone number on our caller ID, he accused me of cheating on him. By now, I had become hypervigilant and paranoid about phone calls. If a salesman or wrong number called, I made sure I deleted the number from the caller ID. I didn't want to get beaten again.

So I grabbed Ruby in my arms and made my way down the busy street to the nearest phone booth. I inserted the coins and punched the corroded silver buttons.

Mom answered hesitantly, unsure who would be on the other end of the line.

"It's me, Lori," I said. "Mom, I need to come home for a visit. I have a baby. Just so you know, you're a grandma. But I need to come home and visit."

"Sure, honey, we'd love to see you," Mom's voice said, betraying her hesitancy and surprise.

When I mentioned the idea to Kito, he seemed nonchalant.

"Sure, you can visit," he said, still staring at the television.

So I packed up my bags and hurried back to Pennsylvania with Ruby. While I was home, I had Cantor Abraham perform a naming ceremony on my daughter.

I will never tell Kito, I vowed to myself as I listened to Cantor Abraham's words of blessing.

"May he bless this beloved girl and let her name be with Good Luck and a blessed hour; and may she grow up in good health, peace, and tranquility."

Peace filled my heart. Even if Kito found out and beat me when I got home, I would rest assured that my daughter could never be named in another church.

Now that Mom knew I had Ruby, she was very concerned about our well-being and health. And she had reason to be concerned. After I went back to Florida, I never knew what kind of mood Kito would be in when I came home from work each day. Sometimes, he was in a mild, harmless mood. But other times, if I even looked at him wrong, I got beaten. I spent my forty-five-minute commute dreading his reaction. *Has he been drinking today? Has he come up with some bizarre offense that he thinks I've done? Will he be angry? Or will he be in a rare good mood?*

The uncertainty drove me to the point of despair. After my suicide attempt, I got off the bathroom floor with new determination. I had attempted suicide several times before, but this time was different because *I* was different. Within a week of the suicide attempt, I knew what I needed to do.

The way Kito treats me is not acceptable. I wasn't raised that way and I certainly am not going to have my child raised that way. I need to leave. I need to get out of this situation. And I need to get long-term help.

Chapter 9

But the question remained: *How do I get out?*

For a few days, I tried to figure out the best way to leave. While I pondered, I went back to the shul one last time.

"I am leaving town," I told the rabbi after my decision was made.

"Where are you going?"

"Oh, I'm going to Wilkes-Barre, a small town in Pennsylvania."

"Really? Are you serious? That's where my assignment is. Maybe I'll see you there!"

The fact that Rabbi Kaplan was moving only confirmed my conviction that I needed to leave. I would need to be careful about my escape plan, and I would need help. The first obvious step was calling my parents.

Because Kito was so paranoid about our home phone, I had to leave the apartment and go down the street to even call my mom. She had not heard from me for a while.

Now, I stood in the phone booth, trying to work up my courage. Finally, I dialed the number on the grimy pay phone.

"Hello?" my mom answered tentatively.

"Hello, this is Lori," I said, not waiting for a reply. "I need to come home."

Mom told me she agreed that I should get out of the situation. But she wanted to consult with my dad and see what he said.

"Dad is not home right now," Mom said. "You need to wait until your dad comes home."

So I waited. They called me back within ten to fifteen minutes. They said I could come home.

"I have no money," I said. "I have no way of getting to the airport. I can't buy a ticket."

"We will take care of everything," Dad said. "Don't you worry."

Relief flooded me. It felt so good to have my parents taking care of me again. I knew I had done the right thing. I knew it was time to leave Kito.

Hastily, I packed up my scant possessions and hid them in my closet. Kito was still at work, and I hoped against hope that he wouldn't look in the closet when he came home. I didn't want him to see all the suitcases, which were packed with diapers, clothes, and everything I owned. I couldn't let him see that the drawers and clothes racks were empty. After I packed everything up, I waited for Dad to call.

The minutes seemed like hours, but it was actually less than forty-five minutes before my dad called back.

"I have everything situated," he said. "A car service will pick you up early tomorrow morning. I bought you and Ruby two plane tickets."

I was eager to leave, but I also knew I needed to bide my time. Kito came home from work. It was a normal day. I made him supper and put Ruby to bed. Kito relaxed on the couch for a while, his lanky figure stretched out in apathy as he stared at the TV. Thankfully, today he did not beat me.

Early the next morning, my husband left for work. Under cover of darkness, I snuck out of the house with Ruby. Back to Pennsylvania we came. I left him in 1998. Ruby was almost a year old.

It was winter. When I arrived at the Pennsylvania airport, my mom and dad had a little red coat waiting for Ruby when I got off the plane. They knew that Florida was relatively warm and balmy, and Ruby and I might not be dressed for the Northern cold.

"We didn't know what you would look like," my parents said, sizing me up.

I glanced down, a bit embarrassed. I knew I had come off that plane with bruises and a handprint on my neck. As we drove back to my childhood home, I was deep in thought.

So much had happened since I left this familiar tiny town. While I was away, I had given birth to my first child, placed her for adoption, entered and left an abusive marriage, and given birth to a second baby girl. It seemed like it had been forever, yet it had only been two and a half short years. As a new single mother, I tried to reintegrate into life in Pennsylvania. My parents' love, care, and acceptance of Ruby went a long way in helping my adjustment.

Although my journey forward wasn't easy, I did eventually turn my life around. Even though I'd been away from Pennsylvania for a long time, I reconnected with my beloved therapist from high school. He was still practicing, so I went back and saw him. He and I began working on a lot of things that needed to be dealt with. I was diagnosed with depression, and I finally received the help that I so desperately needed.

After I got settled in Pennsylvania, I tried again to get in contact with Olivia. I called the attorney to let her know my new address. In case the birth parents sent pictures, I didn't want them to get lost in the mail. While I was on the phone with her, I asked about the letter I'd written to Olivia. Despite the paralegal's promises that she would give it to the adoptive parents, I was never sure that she had actually done so. If she had, wouldn't the adoptive parents have contacted me by now?

"Was the letter received and given to the adoptive family and my daughter?" I asked the attorney's office.

"That will be 500 dollars to go into your file and look for it," she replied.

All she wanted was to make some more money off of me.

"Never mind," I said. I knew I couldn't afford $500 just to check.

After I arrived home in Pennsylvania, I felt very much in pieces. Placing a child for adoption had been difficult, but being a young single mom was difficult as well. Raising Ruby by myself was a lonely journey. I was looking for anything that would ground me and that would help me find wholeness. So one Saturday, I walked into Temple Israel, my own Shul. The light of the giant stained-glass window bathed the entire room in gold.

I sat down on the pew and gazed upwards at Rabbi Kaplan. His kippah perched on his head, and his round face glowed in the light of the tall candles behind him. His melodic, familiar voice launched into a comforting singsong as he delivered the traditional chant.

I moved my lips, praying alongside the congregation. Suddenly, I felt like I was home. After many years of struggling with G~d, I felt peace. As I was praying, I began to feel grounded. I felt prepared to pick up the pieces of my shattered life and piece them back together. The expansive stained-glass window looked like a sun, with rays of yellow and white extending outward from the center. I knew that the broken pieces of my life could become a stained-glass window, a windowpane of light.

After the service, Rabbi Kaplan and Cantor Abraham welcomed me kindly. I instantly knew that I finally had somewhat of a family. Martin Luther King, Jr. once said, "Take the first step in faith. You don't have to see the whole staircase, just take the first step." Going back to Shul was my first step of faith. It forced me to reconnect with my roots, my core reason for being. I was glad I was starting to take baby steps toward freedom.

After that, I started attending Temple every Shabbos. I still felt very alone in my community, and I wondered if my community looked down on me for having a biracial baby. But I found a lot of solace in going to shul. Several older ladies were very kind to me, and one in particular really took to me and Ruby. After Shabbos services, she would invite me over to her house to hang out. She'd play with the baby; we'd sit and chat and talk. Her welcoming kindness was a balm that I had not found anywhere else.

Outside my new relationship with my faith, my life continued to be very robotic and lonely. I would go from the house to drop off my daughter for daycare, go to work, and then vice versa. I didn't go anywhere, didn't have any friends, and didn't want to make any friends. None of my childhood friends were still in my hometown. I was very much alone.

One day in 2000, my mom finally said to me, "Listen, you need to get out of this house. You need to go somewhere, do something, socialize, and spend time with others. You can't stay cooped up in the house all the time!"

So that night, I cleaned up and went to the Woodlands, one of the only places in Wilkes-Barre to hang out with locals. Before I went into the club, I got caught up in a conversation with an acquaintance who wanted to date me. I knew that he wanted to date me, but I also knew that my daughter Ruby did not care for him. There was no way I was going to date someone unless my daughter adored him. Plus, I did not like this man romantically. So I was content being just friends. He and I were standing in a group, chatting.

"Lori is Italian," someone in the group was saying.

A guy named Michael walked up and said, "She's not Italian, she's Jewish."

I said, "They know."

I wondered how Michael knew that I was Jewish, so I struck up a conversation with him. I soon learned that he had moved to Wilkes-Barre from New York. Since we'd both lived in New York, we had a lot in common. We continued talking, and my other friends went into the club. But Michael and I headed to his red Amigo instead. He turned up the jazz music and kept right on chatting. I smiled contentedly. I loved the sound of his deep, rumbling voice.

As we continued to talk, I found out that Michael had a variety of hobbies. He was an avid cyclist, known to some as the "King of Retro Jerseys." He was also a speed skater, a USPSA Shooter, and a photographer.

At that, my ears perked up.

"I love photography, too," I said. "I don't have much experience with it, but my mom has always been into art and photography. I'd love to pick up a camera again. How did you get started?"

"I've always been a photographer," Michael replied, "since I was young. It's been a hobby of mine. But after I went to Vietnam to serve on the 173rd Airborne Brigade in Vietnam, I realized that life was short."

I nodded pensively.

"That experience was sobering for me," Michael continued. "When I came back, I realized how important it was to capture every moment of my life. We never know when it may be our last. So I worked hard to capture my life through photography. I restarted my hobby."

I nodded silently. We were quiet for a moment.

"What are your favorite types of photography?" I added.

"I love black and white photography. I especially like fine art and landscape photography."

We were silent again.

"That's great," I said softly.

I was fascinated with Michael. He was very much a gentleman, very kind, very sweet. We talked the entire night.

But as the evening wound down, he did not ask for my phone number. So I didn't give him my phone number and we called it a night. As I went home that night, my mind wandered.

I really enjoyed my evening... I guess my mom was right.

A few weeks later, I was out again at the Woodlands. It was one of my friends' birthdays, and I went to celebrate with her. The buzz of voices, the sounds of music and dancing, and the bright lights of the resort surrounded me. All of a sudden, I felt a tap on my shoulder. I turned around.

"Michael!" I exclaimed, and he wrapped me in a warm embrace.

At that moment, I knew that Michael enjoyed spending time with me the way I enjoyed spending time with him. The rest of the evening, we were inseparable. That day in May 2000, Michael and I realized that we were a couple, and we've been together ever since.

I still think it's crazy how that coincidence happened. I went out that night because my mother told me to, and I ended up meeting Michael. If I had chosen instead to curl up on the couch, I might never have met my true love, best friend, and amazing husband, Michael.

Michael and I began building a family together. He accepted Ruby, and she loved him in return. A few years later, we were married in the Magistrate's office. I hated how utilitarian the ceremony was; I wished it was more lovely, scripted, and beautiful, truly reflecting our love for one another. But it got the job done: Michael and I were wed for life.

Chapter 10

My everyday life with Michael was full of small moments and memories. Every Friday evening, I enjoyed lighting Shabbos candles. On Sabbaths and holidays, I surrounded myself with friends and chosen family. For Passover, I always invited my Jewish and non-Jewish friends to take part in the celebration. I loved the feeling of having people around my table, doing Seder. My birthday usually fell around Passover, so it was always a special time of year for me. Candles gleamed, wine sparkled, and I felt the joy of my childhood all over again.

Together, Michael and I developed our own personal family traditions. Before I met Michael, I used to buy Chinese food on Christmas day. But after I got married, I started making him a traditional Christmas dinner: glazed ham, crumbly stuffing, and steaming green beans. Even though I always kept a Kosher home, I made an exception and made ham for my beloved on Christmas and Easter. And I whipped up his favorite homemade macaroni and cheese–Michael's mom's recipe that I had perfected and made my own.

One Christmas when Ruby was little, my baby was sick and we couldn't figure out what was going on. The doctors sent us to Pittsburgh for testing right over Christmas. We had one appointment before Christmas and another after Christmas. We spent Christmas day in the hotel.

"Where should we go for Christmas dinner?" Michael wondered. "There aren't many places open on Christmas day."

After searching our options, I was elated. "There's an Indian restaurant open," I said. "My favorite! Let's go!"

Michael went along with it, even though he wasn't big on spicy food. I extravagantly ordered food for everyone, but it turned out to be way too spicy.

"Too intense," Michael said, drinking an extra glass of water to wash down the spice. Ruby squeezed her eyes closed and made a face.

After that, neither Ruby nor Michael would eat Indian food. I settled for cooking other comfort foods they enjoyed, like creamy mashed potatoes and homemade mac and cheese.

With Michael's companionship, I raised Ruby. Since it was my first time raising a child within the home, I discovered that motherhood was truly uncharted territory.

All I had was my intuition, values, and love to serve as my guideposts.

Like every mother, I had to make many decisions daily. Some were small, like: *What should I feed my family today?* Some were big, life-changing decisions: *How do I teach my child right from wrong? Am I giving her what she needs?* And alongside all the questions I asked daily about the journey of raising Ruby, I continued to be pestered by the biggest decision of all: *Was adoption the right thing to do?*

I was very open with Michael and Ruby about the daughter I had placed for adoption. I always thought of Olivia as Ruby's sister, and I honestly explained my motives for placing her for adoption. Much of the time, I knew in my heart that my decision to place my daughter for adoption was the right one; I wasn't ready to be a good parent to her, and I wanted to give her a different life.

But just as often, a shadow of grief and regret crossed my path. I struggled with my choice to place Olivia for adoption. I wondered if I was a bad person for not wanting to be a mom yet—for my baby's sake or mine. I wondered if I'd made the right choice.

I hadn't told my mom about Olivia, but I was grateful for her guidance and support as I raised Ruby.

"Mom, I am raising one girl, how did you raise four?" I would ask her.

She would look at me and just smile. "Being a mom is hard," she'd say sometimes. "You have to make many decisions in the course of one day, and you're not always sure you're making the right decisions. Your children will question your choices. But my only advice is to stand by your decisions, no matter what path they may lead you down."

Mom had no idea the magnitude of the biggest parenting decision I'd ever made, the decision I was still doubting, revisiting, and questioning deep in my heart: *Did I do the right thing to give Olivia up for adoption? As her mother, did I make the choice that was truly best for her?*

Mom was still talking. "Sometimes you make decisions that others will agree with, and sometimes you make decisions that others will judge. But they are yours to make. No one can take your journey as a mother for you, but often we moms need to lean on each other and on the others who care about us."

"Yes, Mom," I said, giving her a brief hug. "I'm so grateful for your support."

But on the inside, I was wavering. Mom had no idea just how desperately I feared that judgment. And I feared that if Mom ever found out my secret, she would be first in line to judge.

I thought about Olivia every day, especially when her birthday rolled around. I wondered where she was and if I would ever run into her.

Are her parents the people that I thought they would be? I wondered constantly. But there was no way to find out. I didn't have any way to find that information. I didn't have access to a computer, and the internet was not what it is now. Even if I had had access to the internet, I never even had the adoptive parents' full names. I only had their first names. They had all my info, but I never had theirs.

Still, I tried to do searches. I went to the library and waited as the computer flickered to life. Then I navigated to the adoption boards for bio parents looking for their children. I typed in all my information.

"Lori Prashker—Adoption," I wrote with shaking fingers.

The processor buzzed as the internet slowly registered my request. Slowly, information started popping up. I actually could find my name and some other records that included my info. But I could never find anything that connected me to Olivia.

I wonder if they changed her name, after all, I thought as I closed down the computer monitor. *They promised they would keep her name the same, but I wonder if they changed it after all...*

Disappointed, I headed for home once again.

Michael stood by me during every struggle and all my successes. That is true friendship and true love. With Michael at my side, I created a successful career and family life.

In 2005, Michael and I rebirthed ShadowCatcher Photography. Together, we began creating memories for family, friends & clients. Michael focused on fine art shots, while I specialized in headshot & portrait photography, and photography for events and weddings.

Since I had lost so many of my early photographs and my parents' wedding photos in the fire, it was meaningful to me to capture footage of weddings. I loved doing photojournalism for these couples: capturing the rapturous joy, the tender tears, and the depth of emotion that these couples shared with their families and friends.

Over time, I realized that taking photos wasn't enough. I wanted to become more involved in the wedding ceremony itself. Some of the weddings I photographed were beautiful, well-scripted services, but others were utilitarian, like my own wedding to Michael. I often felt a prick of regret when I thought of the simple service that had united Michael and me in marriage. I wanted to help other couples craft custom-made services that suited their unique needs. I dreamed of writing beautiful wedding ceremonies for all of the couples I would marry.

I loved writing, and I wanted to incorporate the art and craft of writing into the wedding ceremony. I decided that it was time to become a wedding officiant so that I could write beautiful ceremonies for other couples. That's why I started Ceremonies by Lori.

I originally became ordained in 2011 with the Universal Life Church Ministry and continued my education to become an ordained "Rabbi" in June 2013 with the American Marriage Ministries. I became a Certificated Wedding Officiant through the Wedding Merchant Business Academy. I would always tell my couples, "I am a one-stop-shop... Officiant, Photographer, Hair & Makeup Squad & so much more!!! Give me a list; I will get it done, on time or faster!"

For my day job, I worked a temp job because the money was better and I could work my hours the way I wanted to and could. I was a legal secretary for twenty years, a receptionist, and a Therapeutic Services Support (TSS) for a few months. I worked at Sally Mae for a year and did secretarial work. Later, I became a Paralegal at Lehman Law, PC. I prided myself on high productivity and efficiency in my work.

In my busy life, I also took time for service to others. After a bout with breast cancer, I became a part of I Picture Hope, an organization that offers free photo shoots to men and women who survived or are fighting cancer. I eventually took over the organization.

A few years later, Dr. Sheri, a fellow breast cancer survivor and founder of the Live Today Foundation, planned a retreat and a cruise for breast cancer survivors. When I heard about the trip, I said, "I will volunteer to do free photo shoots for every breast cancer survivor that is a part of this retreat."

Dr. Sheri was touched. "I Picture Hope really allows cancer survivors to appreciate the beauty they cannot see," she told me. "There's something special about the way you photograph them. When they see their photos, they're like, 'OMG that's me?' Lori, you have the knack to bring out the inner beauty, so these photos look magnificent—even in their baldness, when they feel they look their worst."

In addition to multiple businesses and nonprofits, working at my temp job, and raising Ruby, I did graphic art and built websites in my free time. In almost every way, my life was full and complete. I was happy and successful.

But the shadow of grief never left me. I longed to hear news about Olivia, to know that my growing girl was okay. Most of all, I wanted my daughter to understand the reasons I had placed her for adoption. My heart ached for her, hoping that she didn't feel rejected and alone. I wanted her to know that I did what I did because I loved her. Michael, Ruby, and I all knew that I loved her deeply and thought about her daily. And I wanted Olivia to know that, too.

Chapter 11

The worst part about it was the silence. For many years, I ran from telling my story because of the shame. I was ashamed of myself and afraid of shaming my family. Even though I was very open and honest about the adoption with my husband and daughter, I was not open about it with the rest of my family. I still did not want to tell them what had really happened. There was so much stigma.

For many years, the nightmare of shame, pain, and loneliness did not leave me. Because of the fear and stigma surrounding adoption in the Jewish community, it is fair to say I lived through one of my worst fears. I experienced brutal shame and excruciating pain, missing a piece of myself, for many years.

As the years passed, I didn't talk about this experience. I ran from my pain. I knew that the conversation around abortion and adoption was so frequently weighed down by judgments, opinions, and agendas. Particularly in the Jewish community, my own community. The cost of this was that my pain became invisible, just like the pain of so many other women in the Jewish community. My needs were invisible, too.

I still hung onto hope that my own family's response would somehow be different. One day, I could remain silent no longer. I don't remember how it came up. I must have been hemming and hawing when I finally blurted out, "I have another child that I placed for adoption years ago."

"We know," Dad said, his voice icy and laced with shame. "We've known that for years."

My parents knew?! I screamed inwardly. *How did they know? They did not find out from me!*

"How?" I blurted out loud.

"We found out while cleaning out the bedroom you were staying in. One of the papers you left behind mentioned your daughter Olivia."

It was still sinking in that they had known all along, yet they had never said anything to me. My mom's voice interrupted my reverie.

"How dare you? How could you have given away my grandchild?" Mom stared at me with pained, hardened eyes. "I never forgave you for giving away my grandchild."

The words seemed to cut like a knife. I had moved all the way to Florida to keep my mother from shame and embarrassment. But now, she was turning on me, shaming me, embarrassing me in front of the entire family.

My hopes for acceptance were dashed. With great sadness, I realized that my own Jewish community and my own family were just as judgmental as the next person. I felt bad for myself, but deep down, I also felt bad for my mother. My decision to place my daughter for adoption not only affected my life, but my family's as well. I had hidden a huge part of my life for so many years, and talking about it wasn't easy. As much as my parents loved me, I knew they were very upset and disappointed in me.

My community was disappointed as well. I began to be bullied by a member of the congregation I loved so deeply. I could hear the whispers: "Lori is a bad mother. She gave up her daughter for adoption." One day, a group of friends told me this to my face.

Is it true? I asked in my weaker moments. *Should this choice really be something I should be ashamed of? Does placing my baby for adoption make me a bad mother? Doesn't it demonstrate the highest self-sacrifice possible in motherhood—putting my baby's needs ahead of my own comfort and convenience?*

But I wasn't strong enough yet to stand up for myself. I couldn't yet say these things out loud. Haunted by memories of childhood bullying, I did not speak up for myself. I just left the shul and didn't come back for many years.

But in the silence, away from my congregation, the conversations still stuck with me. The whispers and the words of my very own mother haunted my dreams. Years later, her statement still stings. That's part of my trauma. I took the road less traveled, made a courageous choice to save my child's life, and I was only punished for it.

After my mother's scathing words, I became even more grateful for my tradition of inviting my chosen family to my Passover celebrations. I was thankful for their love and acceptance of me, but I was also thankful for the opportunity to offer family love to people who didn't have supportive families of their own.

One day, Ruby's best friend came to me. She looked nervous and fearful. I could tell there was something on her mind.

I gave her my attentive presence and a gentle look of empathy. She opened her mouth and began to speak.

"I am gay," she whispered. Then she went on, "My family is not accepting. They said I am not welcome at home anymore unless I change my sexual orientation. Mrs. Prashker-Thomas, what do I do?"

I put my arm around her shoulder.

"Thank you so much for sharing," I said to her. "I am honored that you trusted me with this. I want you to know that when you are around me, you are welcome to be who you are. You will never be alone. You have me. With me, you have a place to stay, food and shelter always."

As we chatted for a few more minutes, I continued, "You will learn to be accepting of who you are, and you will also learn to be accepting of people around you. That's what happened to me. My family was not supportive of my journey of becoming a Jewish birth mother. But through that experience, I learned to extend empathy and understanding to everyone around me, even those who are different. If your family can't be supportive, then your family is not family. Family doesn't have to be blood. Family can be anyone you choose for it to be."

"Thank you, Mrs. Prashker-Thomas," she said. I could tell by the look on her face that she felt genuine peace. "I feel a lot better now."

Despite the strained and painful relationship I sometimes had with my parents, I never took them for granted. I was grateful that my mom and dad still loved me, and I never doubted that.

In January 2009, I could tell my mother was not doing well. Since I lived near my mom, I noticed that something was off.

"I'm not sure what happened to Mom," I told my sisters. "I think she may have had some mini-strokes. She's hallucinating, picking at things. She spends a long time picking at her housecoat, and I ask her, 'What are you looking for?' Then she says, 'I dropped my pills.'"

"Hmm, not normal," my sisters agreed.

"Another time, she said she was playing hide and seek with Ruby," I continued.

"Do you think she needs to go to the hospital?" my sister asked.

"Yeah," I admitted.

Before we took her to the hospital, I sat with Mom and held her hand. Mom had bad rheumatoid arthritis, so holding hands was not something we could do. But the last day before we had to take her to the hospital, I got to hold her hand. That's a memory that I will always have. I remember her skin being very soft. I can remember seeing her veins standing out, as she was so ill. I remembered when I was a little girl holding her hand. It was a very comforting thing.

After she got to the hospital, my sister joined me. We could tell Mom would not be with us much longer. Mom kept making comments about seeing her family members.

She would say, "I'm making my bed, Mom, I'm making my bed."

She would see my older sister, who had passed away many years earlier. We knew she was about to leave us for the world beyond.

"It's okay, you can let go," I reassured my mom. "Dad's going to be okay, we're all going to be okay."

I wasn't sure my dad was going to be okay. I wasn't sure how long he was going to stay with us. But I didn't want Mom to feel like she needed to stay when it was clearly her time to go.

The day she was passing, she was in the ICU, intubated. They took out the tube and stopped the meds and Mom opened her eyes and saw my sister and me. Dad was standing on the other side of the bed, and Mom couldn't see him. Mom kept looking back and forth, her gaunt eyes scanning the room.

"She's looking for Dad," I whispered.

"Dad, come here," I invited. He came and stood right behind us. As soon as Mom saw him, she closed her eyes and passed.

It was one of the most tender moments I had with my mom. After all the pain and trauma, our family was united in love once again.

Chapter 12

After losing my mom, we all grieved. My daughter, Ruby, suffered this loss in her own teenage way. Sometimes, she took out her pain and frustration on me, her mother.

One day, in a flustered teenage moment, Ruby shouted, "I wish you had given *me* up for adoption!"

I knew she didn't mean it; she was just a teenager being reactionary. But it still pricked me in the heart. I loved Ruby to death. I had sacrificed so much to raise her. I wanted her to value the love I had for her, and the determination I'd had to keep her in my life.

I need a parent time out, I muttered to myself, walking briskly to my room. I locked my door behind me, and I could hear Ruby fussing on the other side.

"Ruby, please go," I told her. "I need some time alone."

In the solace of my room, I took some time to breathe and calm down. My pounding heart slowly returned to its normal rate.

I have given her all I can, I said to myself. *And I pray hard for her, even during the times she appears not to want my involvement at all in her life.*

In the silence, I thought about my journey. Placing Olivia for adoption had been excruciatingly painful, and I knew that aborting her would have also brought grief and loss. But raising a child brought its own kind of pain and heartache. Once a woman becomes pregnant, there are no pain-free options. That's why it's so important to have advocates that walk beside young pregnant moms. When you conceive a child, you will always "have your heart go walking around outside your body," as Elizabeth Stone says. Raising a baby guarantees at least some painful times that go along with the joyful ones.

Another source of pain for me was watching Ruby go through the same bullying and exclusion that I had gone through as a child. Ruby was biracial, a first-generation African American. Yet she was also Jewish, and she got teased a lot for that. As Ruby entered her teen years, I began reliving my own childhood bullying.

It wasn't easy being the parent of a fourteen-year-old. I would see what she went through on a daily basis with all of her friends and all of the drama. She would come home and tell me everything that was going on.

"They tease me for being Jewish," she said. "Mom, what do I do?"

"It will get better," I told her. "Believe me, I can relate to what you are going through. I was the outcast in my small school when I was young. I was bullied so much that I tried to end my life three times. Yet by G~d's grace, I am still here today. I persevered to who I am today. You can persevere, too. Just think! After years of bullying and abusive partners, I found your dad! He treats both you and me like queens! Just remember, Ruby, when life seems really, really bad, it can get better."

Ruby sniffed, and I could tell she was paying attention.

"You are who you are and you need to be proud of who you are," I continued. "Keep going with who you are and be yourself. That's how I became the person I am."

"You're so strong, Mom," Ruby said. "I don't know how you do it all."

I smiled. There were so many joyful moments that went along with the heartache of raising my child. Walking this journey with Ruby has not been painless, but it has been very rewarding.

"I love you so much," I replied. "As long as I am breathing, I will love you with all my heart."

In June 2014, my husband and I moved back into the home I grew up in. My dad's Parkinson's was getting worse, and he had fallen several times.

"Under no circumstance do I want to be in a nursing facility, assisted or otherwise," my father said.

To fulfill my father's wishes, my husband and I packed up our apartment and moved into my childhood home.

"It's time to move in with Dad," Michael and I agreed. Finally, after years of strained relationships, Dad was okay with us moving in with him.

Moving back into my childhood haunt felt like coming home. Michael and I chose the back bedroom, my favorite bedroom with the purple shag carpet, as our master bedroom. The view was beautiful as always: green in summer, snow in winter. It was secluded and quiet.

The former master bedroom was not our style, so we later converted it into our gym. We redid the basement, and I converted one corner into a little office for myself. One November day in 2014, I was in my office in the basement. Michael came downstairs with a letter for me.

"You've got mail!" he said with a grin.

I swiveled toward him and took the letter. Tearing it open, I suddenly froze in my seat.

"Dear Ms. Prashker,

"I hope that this letter finds you well. We met in 1996 on March 23rd in Coral Springs, Florida…"

I dropped the card on the floor and began to cry. I didn't even have to finish the letter. I knew immediately it was from Olivia.

My shoulders shook with sobs. I cried. I bawled. Michael stood there looking at me as if I was crazy.

When I could finally speak, I squeaked out, "This is from the daughter that I placed for adoption."

I had been open and honest about Olivia from the beginning of our marriage, so he knew what I was talking about. Michael looked at me in amazement. His face said it all.

"I can't believe it… I can't believe it…" I repeated over and over.

When I finally stopped sobbing, I picked up the card off the floor and read the rest of the words.

"I hope that this letter finds you well. We met in 1996 on March 23rd in Coral Springs, Florida. When I turned 18 years old, my parents gave me a letter that you wrote to me when I was born along with a picture of you. With this said it would mean a great deal to me if you would be willing to make contact with me. I have been thinking a lot about the entirety of the situation and I do not want you to feel obligated to respond and I do not want to cause any unnecessary turmoil in your life. If you do wish to contact me you can reach me by email or regular mail.

"Love always, Anastasia."

Then she included her email and mailing address.

"So what did she say?" Michael asked.

"She wants to get to know me," I said limply.

"So are you going to write her?" he asked.

"Of course!" I sobbed again, this time with excitement. "I'm not going to send her a letter by the USPS. That would take too long! I'm going to email her right away so she knows I am interested in meeting her."

After I sent the email, I spent the rest of the afternoon processing what I had just learned. Facts filtered into my consciousness one by one.

I guess she did get that letter that I gave the paralegal! I thought in delight. I was so grateful I had written it!

The next few weeks were a blur. Opening my email inbox and finding letters from my daughter seemed like a dream. When we Skyped for the first time, I gasped with joy to see her face. My daughter was eighteen and a freshman in college. But I still recognized her from the moment I had held her in my arms. The depth of emotion I felt almost overwhelmed me.

Now I could see that the same irony that characterized the parenting journey was also true of the adoptive journey. Just like parenting Ruby contained both difficulty and joy, being a birth mom would be both painful and very rewarding. I could finally see that there would be joyful moments that went along with the heartache of placing my child for adoption.

Chapter 13

Anastasia and I had several more conversations on Skype, and I tried to take things slowly. But I had some important questions for her.

"How long did you know you were adopted?" I asked.

"I've always known," she said. "My parents were very open about my adoption and read me children's books about adoption. I knew from Day One that I was adopted."

Anastasia had some questions for me, as well. Hard questions.

"Why did you decide to place me for adoption?" she asked directly.

I was as honest as I could be. I didn't want to hide anything from my daughter. "I was not emotionally prepared to be a parent," I said. "Life does not always play out the way you envision it. Circumstances change. Seasons change. People change. I never thought I would be placing a child for adoption, but life caught me off guard. When I found out I was pregnant, I realized I was responsible for your entire life. I didn't want you to suffer emotionally while I got back on my feet. I knew the best choice I could make was to allow you to live with parents who were prepared—right away—to give you the love and support you needed."

Anastasia nodded thoughtfully. "That makes sense," she said.

"But I cried a thousand tears after I said goodbye to you," I went on. "I thought of you every day and hoped to hear from you."

Anastasia nodded again, a faint look of confusion crossing her face. "I wanted to reach out to you before that," she said, "but I thought I'd get in trouble."

"I'm so glad you did," I said, feeling vaguely perplexed. *Why did she think she would get in trouble?*

"I had the best life I could have asked for," Anastasia said.

Over the next few weeks, I continued to wonder, *Why did she think she would get in trouble?* I didn't want to ask her, because we were just starting to talk, and I didn't want to ask such a personal question just yet.

As time went on, Anastasia and her parents made plans to travel to Milford, Pennsylvania to meet me in person. Anastasia and her adoptive parents decided to meet

Michael and me at the historic Hotel Fauchere. As Michael drove the car through the downtown streets that morning, my stomach was in knots.

Will Anastasia be angry with me? Will she ever forgive me? Does she hate me?

I squeezed my hands tightly together, closed my eyes, and listened to the sounds of the traffic. I tried to breathe. To bring myself back to the present.

When we arrived, Anastasia's family was not there yet. Michael and I meandered closer to the historic Italianate-style building and waited. Dark antique shudders stood out starkly against its tall, white face. A lovely lamppost glistened against the last yellow leaves that clung to the sugar maples. In just a few more weeks, the entire place would be lit with Christmas lights.

Inside my chest, I could feel my heart pounding every bit as much as it had the day I had first met the adoptive parents inside the attorney's office. I let my mind wander back to that day.

Back then, I met the adoptive parents to see if I approved of them... now, Anastasia will meet me to see if she approves... if she forgives me... if she still wants to be friends. So many years have gone by since I said goodbye to Anastasia... and in just a few minutes, we will meet again.

Finally, I spotted a middle-aged couple getting out of their car. Beside them was a spitting image of myself.

Anastasia! I murmured under my breath. I moved toward her instinctively, and I could tell the instinct was mutual. Anastasia held out her arms, and I met her with a long embrace. She was tiny when she was born, and she was still less than five feet tall. I felt her hair against my cheek. It was wonderful to hold my baby again.

"It is so good to meet you," Anastasia whispered.

"I am so happy," I replied. Then with a sudden impulse, I whispered back, "Do you hate me?"

"Of course I don't!" Anastasia said, looking me in the eye. "I just want to know you! You're my mother!"

As I stood back and gazed into her eyes, I knew the warmth and love that filled my heart was mutual.

Inside the hotel, the five of us sat down at square tables decked with lovely glasses and candles. The historic portraits on the wall and the swirled silver wallpaper contributed to the sense of awe I felt. My daughter and I were meeting each other against all odds, with love that spanned the decades.

As I sat across from Anastasia, I marveled at the family resemblance.

She looks just like one of us! I thought.

Conversation flowed as we waited for the food. I found out her adoptive parents had given her a love of the outdoors, sent her to camp and college, and instilled a deep loyalty to the Detroit Red Wings.

"It's nice to see you being a fan of something," I said. "I'm also a die-hard sports fan."

The kitchen was taking their time getting our Salmon en Papillote just right.

"Would you like to see her photo album while we wait?" the adoptive mom asked.

"Yes!" I exclaimed. "I'd love to see her as a child."

The adoptive mother started flipping through the baby pictures rapidly.

"You should have already seen these photos," she said, "so let me get to some of the pictures you haven't seen."

I looked at her blankly. "What photos?"

She looked at me inquisitively. "Well, we gave them to the attorney for her to send them to you."

I was baffled. "I never received anything," I said quietly.

Now it was their turn to stare.

"The lawyer told us that you didn't want to see hide nor hair of us after the first three months," the adoptive mother finally said.

"I never said that!"

"But we still sent photos, hoping they'd get through somehow."

Sadness filled me. Photos were so precious to me, and we'd lost all our family's photos in the fire. Now, I realized that I had lost another eighteen years' worth of photos: the photos that my daughter's adoptive parents had tried to send me and wanted to send me. But a selfish attorney had deprived me of my daughter's entire childhood.

In reality, it was not only me that was manipulated by attorneys. To a point, the adoptive family was also manipulated. That set of attorneys was a whole team of people trained to manipulate two different families to do this one thing: give us your money and you'll get this child. Once the transaction was complete, they did not care one bit about maintaining the human connections that were so important to both families.

Now I knew why my daughter kept saying, "I didn't want to get in trouble"! The attorney told the family that I didn't want to see or hear from her. In that instant, I thought about all the angst Anastasia had to go through, thinking she would be in trouble if she contacted me. It took immense courage on Anastasia's part to face the fear of rejection and reach out to me. I was so grateful she did!

"Wow," I said, the news still sinking in. "That's so hard to believe. I'm just glad I get to see them now. Thank you, Anastasia, for having the courage to reach out."

Anastasia was eager to get started with showing me the photos. She turned to a picture of a tiny ballerina twirling in a delicate pink tutu.

"I've been dancing since I was three years old," Anastasia said.

"So have I!" I exclaimed. "I've always loved dancing. Have you had formal training in dance?"

"Yes, I've taken a lot of dance lessons," Anastasia replied.

"Your sister, Ruby, has danced all her life, too," I told her. "She's an amazing dancer. You're going to love meeting her!"

"I can't wait," Anastasia replied.

It was fun to page through the rest of the photo album.

"You inherited the artistic talent from me, too!" I said, pointing to the photograph of Anastasia painting. "Your grandma was an artist. We all love art."

We finished the album, and the food still hadn't come. Anastasia was getting a bit huffy.

"Sorry, I get hangry," she apologized.

"I should be the one apologizing!" I said. "You got that trait honestly, from my side of the family. That's totally a Prashker trait. My father had the bar very high on that one."

She chuckled.

"Yeah, food is my friend," I said.

The food finally came, and the conversation continued to flow. As the afternoon wound down, my belly was full and my heart was content. I could see that the adoptive parents had done a good job. They had taught her that with freedom comes responsibility. They had given her a good sense of humor. They had taken very good care of my daughter. I couldn't have asked for better parents for her.

"I understand that you have always loved me," Anastasia whispered to me as we hugged one last time and went our separate ways.

As we drove home that evening, my mind swirled with emotion. All the way home, I kept saying to my husband, "What if I hadn't made that decision? I missed eighteen years of her life. What did I do?"

He simply reached his hand out, took mine, and gave it a knowing squeeze. As my thoughts faded into silence, I realized I had not made a mistake in trusting these adoptive parents. But I couldn't help the pain of missing out on my daughter's childhood. The what-ifs were terrible.

All those years, it hurt to be so far apart from my daughter, I thought, *but I don't ever wish I had aborted her. It hurt so badly to be away from her—more than I could ever describe—but I couldn't regret loving her.*

Even amidst the worst of it, year after hard year, I never wished I could go back to that abortion clinic and say yes. I always knew that wherever she was, the world was better with her in it. Now that I finally got to hear her voice for the first time, I know, without a doubt, that her life was worth the pain I experienced. If I had to do this again, I would.

I was so grateful for my courage in placing Anastasia for adoption, and I was so grateful for Anastasia's courage in reaching out to me. Her courage allowed for a beautiful new beginning to emerge.

Chapter 14

As the weeks went by, I struggled with the thought, "What now?"

When I met Anastasia, I had been walking on air. It was difficult to describe the emotions I felt. Being reunited with Anastasia was scary, hard, and very beautiful.

Yet now that she had returned to her home state, I wasn't sure what was ahead with our relationship. Was Anastasia's goal to meet me one time, find out who I was, and satisfy her curiosity? Or did she want an ongoing relationship? What about her family? Did they feel threatened by my relationship with Anastasia? After all, they were the ones who raised her. I didn't want to overstep my bounds.

But at the same time, I reasoned, *she is my daughter and a part of my family.*

How would I walk that fine line? Sometimes, the relationship felt a bit strained, only because I didn't want to overstep bounds. I tended to step too far back, but that's where I felt comfortable as I navigated this awkward new relationship. I wanted to leave space for her to enjoy her adoptive family who had given her the amazing life I always wanted for her.

I finally settled on texting Anastasia a simple greeting every morning.

"Good morning, I love you."

"Hey, have a great day, thinking about you."

If she replied, we would continue the conversation, texting or talking every single day. But at the same time, I tried to keep my distance.

That March, I was delighted to receive an invitation to Anastasia's birthday party. For the first time since the day she was born, I would be with her on her birthday. At last, I would get the privilege of watching her blow out her birthday candles.

The atmosphere was festive when I arrived. The bright yellow and purple of the tablecloth and centerpiece matched the flashy colors of the picture on the wall—and reminded me of the vivid colors of the paintings on my own office wall back home.

Anastasia's entire adoptive family was there: aunts, uncles, and cousins. Even her grandma and great-grandma were there, grinning with joy. I exchanged greetings all around. Everyone was delighted to meet Anastasia's birth mom.

When we ate the cake, I sat next to Anastasia at the table. She had a tiny round chocolate cake with a single red candle. As she bent to blow out the flame, her cousins clapped. I grinned with joy. This moment almost made up for all the 18 years I had missed.

Later, we all gathered in the living room to watch her open presents and read her cards. The bright orange cabinet and the turquoise vase in the sitting room matched the collection of colorful gift bags, bright cards, and vibrant, eye-catching tissue paper in the gift bags. My heart felt bright, too.

Anastasia's face glowed from ear to ear as she opened the necklace and bracelet I gave her. She sat on her adoptive mom's lap, her mom peeking over her shoulder as she read her cards. Afterward, everyone passed around the cards and gifts, admiring the messages and sentiments included.

This is true family, I thought. *Anastasia has been happy.*

As I left, I wanted to express one more time my gratefulness to Anastasia's adoptive parents.

"You gave her the best life that she could have, and I will forever be thankful for that," I told them. "You are an amazing family for my daughter. I am incredibly thankful for everything you have done for Anastasia."

As time went on, Ruby had the chance to meet Anastasia as well. Their sister bond developed slowly, going through the hiccups that all siblings experience as they navigate their relationships. The two of them look tremendously similar, even though their skin tone is different. My father's genes were very strong.

The sisters allowed their relationship to develop organically, over time, until they grew an amazing, close sister relationship. Even though the parent-child relationship can be difficult—jealousy can arise—the sibling relationship is different. Anastasia and Ruby can have any kind of relationship they want, and for that, I'll always be grateful.

As Anastasia and I kept in touch, Anastasia brought up an important question.

"Do you know who my biological dad is?" she asked one day.

"No, I honestly don't," I said. "That was one of the things that stressed me out when you were born: that I didn't know who the father was. Like I said before, I wasn't making the best choices at the time."

"I understand," Anastasia replied. "But I'd still like to know who he is."

"You could do some research on Twenty-Three and Me," I suggested.

"Great idea!" Anastasia replied. "I will work on that right away!"

One day, I was lounging in a lawn chair at a USPA competitive shooting match, watching my husband get ready to compete. Other competitors were lined up in their athletic gear, taking aim at the blue barrels. The sun glared down at me, and the noise of the shooting almost obscured the faint sound of my phone ringing.

Whipping it out of my pocket, I saw on the screen that it was Anastasia. I knew right away what she was calling about.

She has answers about her father, I thought.

Immediately picking up the call, I heard Anastasia's voice.

"Hey, can we talk?" she asked.

"Sure," I said. "Give me a sec, I'm on my way to a quiet space." *Good luck finding a quiet space at a shooting range,* I told myself sarcastically.

Once I'd found a secluded spot, I said out loud, "Hey, what's up?"

"I solved the mystery. I found a relative of my birth father, and she helped me find my biological father." Anastasia proceeded to tell me the name of the man who had fathered her. "Do you remember him?" she finished.

"Unfortunately, no," I replied. "I don't remember him. That's not something I'm proud of. I do not want to contact him or for him to contact me."

"I understand, and I will make that request," Anastasia said.

"But what is most important to me is that you have answers," I added. "It's good for you to reach out and find him."

As I hung up, I felt nervous, but at peace. After we got home from the shooting range, I looked up the biological father's name on the internet. I shook my head.

Still don't remember him at all, I thought. *And he's totally not my type. I wonder why I ever hooked up with him.*

Later, Anastasia told me that she'd made contact with her biological father, and that they spoke from time to time. I was very grateful that Anastasia was slowly piecing together her biological heritage.

There was one more piece of the puzzle for Anastasia, one more family she needed to meet: mine. For me, that would be the hardest. But I knew that I needed to finally come clean with my family. I needed to be very open about my daughter, Anastasia, and how proud I was of her.

It was Thanksgiving, and I wanted to make sure my daughter knew my dad. My mom had said she could never forgive me, and I was sure my dad felt the same way, though he had never voiced it. But despite my fears, that Thanksgiving Day, I announced the news.

"We are going to have a brief Skype with my biological daughter, Anastasia," I said.

From the way my father twisted his napkin, I could tell he was uncomfortable. But it was time for me to start pushing past my discomfort and others' discomfort in order to do what was right: speak up.

When the screen flickered on a few minutes later, my dad, my sisters, and their children gathered around the computer. Everyone greeted Anastasia. The look on Dad's face was priceless.

"She very much looks like our side of the family," he breathed. "She looks like *me!*"

"It's like looking in a mirror, isn't it, Dad? The family genes are strong."

Dad was smiling from ear to ear. Like most Jewish older men, my dad was very resistant to showing emotion until he got older. But now that we lived with him, we would occasionally see him shed a tear. When we were watching a movie, I would look over and see him crying quietly. And now, he was not trying to hide the joy that glowed on his face.

Whenever Anastasia visits our town, she gets together with me, Ruby, and Michael. Thankfully, she came for a weekend while Dad was still alive. Since we were living with Dad in my childhood home, Dad and Anastasia got to spend the weekend together. When Dad and Anastasia shook hands and hugged for the first time, I felt a sense of completion that I had not known before. Finally, my precious daughter was accepted by my own father before he died.

Chapter 15

Eventually, most of my family met Anastasia and welcomed her into their lives. I knew that others close to me would not be as accepting of my choice to place for adoption. Beyond a shadow of a doubt, I knew that people in my community were still so judgmental. I knew this because they talked about it constantly. Once, I was conversing with a lady whose daughter and family were adopting a beautiful baby girl.

"I'm sure the child won't be Jewish," the mom complained. "This is a disappointment to my family and friends, and our lineage will be damaged."

She cares more about what others think than about becoming a grandmother to this precious girl, I thought.

"That child was given up at birth and discarded like yesterday's trash," the mother went on. Those were her exact words.

I caught my breath; I was mortified. Not only did I cringe at the term "give up," but I also knew that most birth parents were not "throwing away" their children. They were making a courageous choice to place their child with a loving family who was prepared to give the child the best opportunities possible. It was a heart-wrenching decision, an unselfish choice to think about the child's future rather than about the parent's emotions.

I decided to place my daughter for adoption because I could not take care of myself emotionally, I thought. *I knew that she deserved the best upbringing possible. I agonized over this decision for many months, even after choosing her adoptive parents. I did NOT throw her away!*

Conversations like this one just reinforced my fear of speaking up about my story. Because of the stigma, I kept my story as quiet as I could in my community.

Until one cold December day in 2016. I was sitting at my computer working, even though it was 6:00 a.m. on Christmas Eve. Taking a break from work, I navigated to the webpage of a Jewish magazine that I enjoyed reading. I scrolled quickly past the author's bio, which said the article was written by Erica Pelman, the founder of an organization called In Shifra's Arms that helped young Jewish women with unexpected pregnancies. Her nonprofit for Jewish birthmothers was the only one in the United States. But I didn't see this; my eyes darted immediately to the fascinating content of the story.

The article was about a young Jewish woman who was pregnant and needed to make a decision about placing her child for adoption or having an abortion. She didn't want to tell anyone. She kept everything hush-hush. *Just like me!* I thought eagerly. As my eyes rushed down the page, I felt like I was reading my story all over again.

The world around me was still dark and silent that Christmas Eve morning. I sat in the computer chair, crying. I had been seen, understood, and validated for the first time in my life. That woman was telling my story. Even though it was still Christmas Eve at 6:00 a.m., I knew I needed to speak with this author, as quickly as possible.

"Your article really struck a chord with me," I wrote to her. Then I sent the email, hoping to receive a response after the holidays. In less than thirty minutes, I had an email in my inbox from Erica.

"Lori, when I get back from vacation, we need to talk."

"Okay," I replied simply, intrigued but nervous.

I had no idea what new vistas were about to open up to me in my life. Erica reached out to me when she got back from vacation. Erica Pelman had kind eyes, straight brown hair, and a demeanor that showed both compassion and urgency. In her gentle presence, I told my entire life story.

"We need to get you involved," Erica concluded when I finished. "I would love for you to be a member of our board—and to tell your story. Other women in crises need to hear your story."

I only nodded silently. *Am I ready? Can I do this?*

Erica continued, "There are many other women in your shoes. We recently got a call from Dara. She called the ISA Helpline, pregnant from a casual sexual relationship with her roommate. She immediately told her In Shifra's Arms counselor that she did not want to abort and that she wanted to explore adoption. But when she told the baby's father, a twenty-something law school student, about her wishes, he said he would refuse to sign adoption papers (making adoption legally impossible). He didn't want to raise the baby either. He insisted on abortion and brutally asserted that he would 'make her life hell' if she didn't. After weeks of fighting with him, facing a lifetime of being tied to him through the baby, Dara acquiesced to an unwanted second-trimester abortion.

"Aside from the abuse clearly present in the story, the notion that it is better to abort than place a baby for adoption is a common belief in our Jewish community. The often-unstated understanding is that placing your child for adoption means you are a bad mother or a bad father—you are shameful. Rather than be a bad mother or father, many women conclude it's better not to have the child at all."

"Unfortunately, I totally agree with you," I said to Erica. "The shame is so strong. When it comes to birth parents in the Jewish community, we are not discussed. We don't exist. I do not exist within the community. I *do* exist, but it is not talked about."

"True," Erica said. "Much of the Jewish community is focused on abortion access, and for many reasons, this is important. But what about our community's moral obligation to support women who choose to continue their pregnancies—even in the most difficult of circumstances? What about their needs? Sadly, for some, offering abortion access is a way of getting off the hook. Friends and loved ones advise, 'You can just abort—don't ask me to help you with diapers, your career, childcare, or long-term emotional support.... If you feel sad about your loss, you are just being too emotional.' This is the opposite of being truly pro-choice. We need to be willing to be there, with compassion, for women in the process of the decision and as they deal with the ramifications of whatever decision they make."

"Yes," I agreed. "In the Jewish community, if you are a couple who is adopting a child, you are looked on extremely favorably because you have helped an 'underprivileged' child. You are lauded for that. Yet if you are on the other end of the equation—like me—you are stigmatized and rejected. Nothing in the Scriptures says not to place a child for adoption. It's just decided... understood... in the Jewish community. I'm not saying that adoption is all roses and butterflies. But when parenting is not a good option, then women need to know that adoption can have huge benefits... not only for the baby but also for the woman who can live the rest of her life without the regret of an unwanted abortion."

"And it benefits the Jewish community as a whole," Erica said. "At the same moment that you were pregnant with a baby that you couldn't raise, another Jewish woman was yearning to conceive and was unable. Your baby brought joy to another Jewish family. This dichotomy happens every single day. Yet the shame and stigma scare women away. As far as I am concerned, this taboo is meant to be broken. And I think your story is an important part of that process. You have a powerful story, one that needs to be shared."

"I'll think about it," I said.

As I pondered my conversation with Erica, I knew it was time. If I had shared my story earlier, there might have been too much pain and too much angst. People would not have felt my deliverance, the knowledge that there is always a way out. But now, through my relationship with Anastasia, I was realizing I didn't have to feel ashamed.

The timing of my conversation with Erica could not have been more perfect. Now, I could go forward and share my story with boldness.

I was ready. My voice needed to be heard. Every day, all around me, birth mothers were being marginalized. It was time to start speaking out more publicly about the stigma and pain of living in a Jewish community with this secret. I started by speaking out to my friends, even when they were not receptive.

I joined In Shifra's Arms as the vice-chair of the board, and I felt empowered to share my story. I started to appear in videos for In Shifra's Arms, telling my story.

"Life doesn't fit into neat little boxes," I said. "I know all too well the world of dark secrets. But I refuse to stand in the dark anymore. I am not ashamed of my choices, and I invite every Jewish pregnant woman in crisis to know that she doesn't have to be alone.

"If I can make it better for the next woman, I will do whatever it takes. I am ready to bust the taboo, tell the truth about my pain, face the fears, and challenge the stigma. I want to shower love and devotion on any woman going through what I went through and on our community as a whole.

"Like many Jews, I am proudly pro-choice. I didn't need anyone to make my choice for me, nor do I need to make the choice for others. But I did need someone to walk along my journey and there are many other women who do, too. And that's what In Shifra's Arms can do for you."

Telling my story was very rewarding. Erica pushed me to continue telling it until it felt like second nature to me. I'm grateful that she did, because I wouldn't be where I am today without her. With her support, I arranged my very first speaking engagement: at my own temple.

After being bullied years ago at my shul, I had returned to my synagogue and was meeting with my congregation. I'd returned with a new determination to speak out whenever I saw someone being treated unfairly. Now, it was time to speak up for myself, as well. Rabbi Kaplan gave me permission to speak at Temple Israel in Wilkes-Barre.

"Because you are the vice-chair of the board of ISA, we are happy to have you," he said. "You can do the D'var Torah."

Neither of us realized how little he knew of my story, and how shocked Rabbi Kaplan, the congregation, and the President of the board would be when they heard my unexpected story.

Chapter 16

On January 21, 2017, the day I was scheduled to speak, I stood in front of the congregation, my heart pounding. It was now or never. I cleared my throat and began.

"Good Shabbas!

"As Rabbi stated, my name is Lori Prashker-Thomas and I am Vice-Chair of the non-profit organization In Shifra's Arms: Jewish Support for the Pregnant Woman.

"In Hebrew, the word for compassion, rachamim, comes from the word for womb, rechem. At ISA, we believe there is no expression of compassion more Jewish than reaching out to women struggling with unplanned pregnancies and offering loving support. Our mission is to help struggling pregnant women build a positive future for themselves and their children. We offer both counseling and practical resources throughout pregnancy and after birth as needed.

"While we offer this support, we affirm the fact every woman needs to make choices about her future for herself. Our counseling is client-led rather than formulaic, conducted by a counselor with extensive professional training. We treat all women with the same kindness, compassion, and respect they deserve, whatever their circumstances or choices they end up making. We are a non-partisan, social service organization. Our supporters come from diverse political and religious perspectives, including secular and Orthodox, pro-choice and pro-life, and many people 'in-between.' We come together to ensure that every woman can access our support if she wants it."

Then I launched into the most difficult part: my story. As I talked, I stood at the pulpit, looking at people, trying to see their reactions. Sometimes I say things for shock value, and I wanted to see how I was being received. On the front row, I saw an eighty-year-old woman in tears, listening to my story.

"The ending of my story is definitely unique in the Jewish community," I wrapped up the speech, "but the beginning is not. Every day, some Jewish women find themselves pregnant and vulnerable for a whole variety of reasons. Along with many Jews, I am proud of being pro-choice. I didn't need anyone to make my choice for me, nor do I want to make another's choice for them. However, I did need people to walk alongside me on my journey. For me, and too many others, that support just was not there. But it doesn't have to be that way.

"This week's Parsha, we read about Shifra and Puah, the heroic midwives who stand up for the Hebrew women and their babies against Pharoah. In those dark days of slavery in Egypt, all of the Jewish people must have felt both powerless and hopeless. I imagine how Shifra would have brought comfort and tenderness as she cared for each pregnant Israelite. She could not change the circumstances around them. Yet her indomitable faith in the future must have empowered and strengthened each woman who sought her help.

"In Shifra's Arms is the only Jewish organization in the United States dedicated to helping vulnerable pregnant women to help them to create a positive future for themselves and their children. We are a small non-profit but work with women across the United States. Jewish women deserve to know that they can count on our community during pregnancy and afterwards. They need to be cared for, whatever choice they make, but especially amid the changes and challenges they will face if they raise their children or after they place for adoption. I am grateful that now our community can offer the support I wish I could have had."

After my presentation, the eighty-year-old woman came up to me. I knew her from synagogue; she would sit in the front row in every service.

"Your story was so powerful, and I can relate," she said simply.

From which angle can you relate? I wondered. *I know for a fact that I am not the only Jewish birth mom out there.*

Afterward, a few people said, "Oh my goodness, that's amazing." But most people were reluctant.

"We didn't expect the story we got," they said. "We can't do this again."

They never asked me back.

Back home, I thought again about the older lady's words, "I can relate." I thought of the conversations I'd had with other Jewish birth parents. Some Jewish birth moms who have the baby, deal with what they have to deal with, come back, and it's never discussed. It's almost like being shunned.

The shame and stigma in their lives are so severe that they never disclose to their other children that they have another child. Perhaps they want to forget the reason they had another child. Everyone has their reasons. But a lot of the reasons are imposed by a shame-based society.

After the speech in the synagogue, I told Michael, "I am being shunned now. And shunning isn't even a thing within our community. The Amish do shunning, but Jews don't. Now I know what it feels like. I feel like I have to deny that part of my life so my community doesn't have to hear about it and answer questions about it. So they don't have to feel bad about themselves."

"Do you regret speaking in the synagogue?" Michael asked.

"Absolutely not," I said. "Sometimes, you have to rock the boat a little bit."

As I started telling my story, I met a lot of resistance. When I approached the leader of another nearby synagogue about telling my story, a board meeting was called to discuss the issue. Finally, they told me their answer: no. I heard that members of the board had said, "Nobody wants to hear that!"

That synagogue is supposed to be more open, LGBTQ+ friendly, and accepting, I thought. *Yet they say that "nobody would be interested in my story"? Hmmm...*

It was hard to hear that my small, insular community wanted nothing to do with my story. I felt the stigma and invisibility. I knew it would be difficult to speak up, but I knew it was important. I was no longer a people-pleaser, cowering in front of the bullies' wishes. I had found my backbone.

I continued to hear conversations that shamed birth mothers, but now I wasn't afraid to speak up. I was oohing and aahing over a new baby that some acquaintances had adopted.

"Mazel Tov," I congratulated. "That's great, congratulations." I'm all about the babies!

But in the course of the conversation, the topic of birth parents came up. I asked, "Oh, have you reached out to the birth parents?"

One parent said, "I wish that they never existed."

I looked at them. They didn't know my background.

"Do you have any idea who I am?" They knew who I was, but clearly hadn't heard my story.

"I am a Jewish birthmother."

They looked at me and said, "Oh." They didn't know what to say.

Being shunned for telling my story only reinforced my conviction that this was a message that needed to be shared. If I could make life easier for even one stigmatized mother, it would be worth it. I never knew who might be listening to my story—like that eighty-year-old woman. Even though my story was not very well received in my community, I knew I needed to become more vocal.

A friend suggested that I tell my story on the internet. It would give my message an even wider reach. There are already many adoption-related stories from the perspective of the adoptee's trauma or the birth parent's joy. But there are few stories from the point of view of the birth mother. As I thought about this, I was getting very emotional. I decided to reach out to a friend who is a PR person.

"I need to ask you because I know you'll tell me the truth," I said to her.

"You need to do this, get your story out there, and keep it separate from your other ventures. What do you think about trying TikTok?"

"What do I know about TikTok?" I wondered aloud. "I'm not a teen!"

But I tried it anyway. I started telling my story in three-minute increments. It was really interesting to see who commented, who did not comment, and what they were saying. I got a lot of pushback from the Jewish community. Yet I knew it was worth it.

I realized that I was one of the first to outwardly speak on this issue. Adoption in the Jewish community is common; lots of Jewish people adopt. But in the adoption conversation, I am an anomaly. Jewish women don't place children for adoption, and if they do, it is never spoken about. Yet clearly, people were watching my videos. My content was hitting a nerve.

I laughed when I updated my friend: "TikTok and I are not friends! But now, I am getting a lot of views (for me), like around1000 views."

"That's great!" my friend encouraged me. "It's not about how many follow you, but how many watch the video. Each of them may tell others in their lives. You have no idea how wide and far your story is spreading!"

Erica had one more idea for me.

"You need to write a book," she said.

"Hmmm," I said to her.

"I'm serious. You need to write a book. More people need to hear your story—young and old."

I excitedly began the process of publishing my book. In preparation for its release, I began doing author events and speaking even more openly. Even Rabbi Kaplan wrote a supportive message for my book publicity package. Through the experience of having foster children, he had mellowed; his thoughts and ideas had changed a lot.

As he and his wife had raised several foster children, the rabbi and his family had learned the importance of discussing and connecting with the birth parents of their kids. They became even more kind, open, and understanding toward me.

As I prepared to release my book, Rabbi Kaplan wrote, "When we asked Lori to speak, we did not know her story. We knew her family story but not her story of being a Birth Mother and everything behind the decision. Very powerful and moving story and amazing the way she intertwines her story with Shifra and Puah's story...She makes you think!"

I had no idea about the exciting events that were about to interrupt my book project, the world scene, and my personal life. But they were about to shake me up in a good way, propelling my project forward in ways I could not yet imagine.

Chapter 17

For a few years, life continued as normal. On our tenth wedding anniversary, on the eighteenth anniversary of our life together, Michael and I renewed our vows. We held a beautiful, traditional Jewish wedding ceremony under a lovely chuppah that my sister had needlepointed. As Rabbi Kaplan performed the ceremony, my heart glowed with happiness.

But in 2020, my life was turned upside down. First, I was in a car accident in March. Though the car was totaled, I walked away with only minor injuries. As the world imploded with the pandemic, I recovered from my aches and pains at home. Periodically, I continued to attend checkups at the doctor and chiropractor, just to make sure I was okay.

One day, I started to feel some unusual pain. My jaw was really bothering me, but I thought it was the car accident. Additionally, my rheumatoid arthritis had really gone into a spiral after the accident because of the trauma. So I assumed I was just having a flare.

On May 2, the severe pain in my mouth and jaw combined with a high fever. It was so severe that I headed to the office of my primary care provider. My pain threshold is really high, so if I start complaining, there's a problem.

My doctor immediately sent me to Geisinger South Hospital for a scan of my jaw. After the scan, my husband drove me home. While I was waiting for the results, I lay down to rest.

My sister called me and said, "You need to go to the hospital."

"I don't want to go to the ER or the hospital," I said. "Especially not to Geisinger Hospital—they told me to stay away from the hospital."

"You're really sick, Lori," she said, trying to knock sense into my head.

"It's just my rheumatoid arthritis," I said. "Or maybe the car accident."

Instead of going to the hospital, I fell asleep. I slept from 11:00 a.m. to 6:00 p.m. That's not like me. I never sleep that long in the middle of a Saturday.

When I woke up, I was in such severe pain I took my sister's advice. Michael jumped into the car and drove me to the hospital. At the Emergency Department, I was shuffled into an outdoor tent where I was greeted by people in white hazmat suits.

"You are a potential COVID-19 patient," they told me.

When they took my temperature, it was over 103 degrees.

"Stand right here, we need to wait until we have a COVID room available for you," the nurse told me.

I began crying hysterically. Not even Michael was allowed to enter with me past the COVID tent. It was just me, and I was so sick that I didn't know what was going on. All I knew was that I was not feeling well.

I stood outside for I don't know how long. Finally, when I got a room, I called my husband.

"Go home," I said. "I'm being admitted. I don't really have any other info to go on. Go get something to eat." Even though I was so sick, I was still worried about him.

That's one of the last things that I remember. I've been told that a scan of my lungs showed some changes similar to those that accompany COVID-19. Eventually, the doctors discovered that I had a severe head and neck infection, so they put me on antibiotics. But even the neck infection did not explain the amount of pain I was in or how sick I had become.

Saif Abdulateef, DMD, Attending Physician of Oral and Maxillofacial Surgery, was just finishing his shift when I was diagnosed. He took one look at how sick I was and realized something was off.

"There's something else going on. Her pain for what we have diagnosed is not right."

He immediately volunteered to stay another shift and care for me.

Two days later, they diagnosed me with Ludwig's Angina, which is often misdiagnosed. Ludwig's Angina is a type of bacterial infection that occurs on the floor of the mouth, under the tongue. It often develops from odontogenic sources and if not caught in time can be deadly.

Most people don't recover from Ludwig's Angina, But Dr. Abdulateef fought for my life. The 1,300 pages of notes from my hospital tell how he fought for me when I hung between life and death. The infection was so severe that I had become septic. The doctors intubated me to protect my airways and took me into emergency surgery. They operated on me three times in one week, put in three Penrose drains in my neck, and gave me strong antibiotics to fight the infection.

I lost about fourteen days of my life because of fever, surgeries, and intubation. When I finally woke up, I had no idea what was going on. All I knew was that I was missing teeth, my throat, mouth, neck, and head hurt, and I could not seem to form sentences. I had no recollection of the past fourteen days. It was terrifying.

Dr. Abdulateef and his team checked on me three times a day and tried to make sure I was okay. Three of the hospital residents took me under their wings and tried to make me feel as comfortable as they could each and every day. They told me that I was on the upswing. But I knew I had a long way to go. I felt frightened and very much alone.

Some days, I lay in bed and cried in confusion and fear. Not being able to speak and being scared to swallow was tremendously frightening. The doctor and three residents tried to comfort me as best as possible. One resident knew I was Jewish, and he would wish me a good Sabbath. He'd sit with me and pray a little bit with me on Sabbath.

Every day during rounds, the OMFS team took photos of my mouth, jaw, and neck as they did every day to follow my progress. One morning, I had had enough of the residents coming into my room and taking photos of me. They weren't even using the camera right!

I squeaked out, "You're using your camera wrong!!!"

They stared at me in surprise.

"What did you say?"

I felt I was screaming in my head, but they could not hear me. I repeated myself. "I am a professional photographer, and you are using your camera wrong."

For so long, I had felt I had no control over anything that was happening to me. But my assertion that I could help them use their equipment correctly meant a great deal to me. From then on, when the team came in to do rounds and take mandatory photos, they asked me for approval of their photos. It was a very tiny way for me to gain control over a situation where I had no control. One small triumph for me!

When I was finally able to talk and understand what was going on, Dr. Abdulateef and his team did everything they could to try to explain what happened because I had no recollection.

"If you had not come into the emergency room when you did, it is very likely you would not be alive today," the doctor emphasized.

My room was on the corner of the hall which separated the COVID-19 section of the ICU and the non-COVID sections. Every day, I watched the COVID patients coming in on ventilators. Then days later, I would see those same patients being wheeled back out in metal boxes. I knew what that meant.

Every day, I wondered, "Will that box come for me next?"

One night, in a vision, my late dad came and saw me. He yelled at me, "It's not your time. You need to go back." Then he left. Typical Dad. He seemed to think I still had a job to do here on earth.

Every time I saw a metal box go by, I would say Kaddish to the best of my ability because I could not remember any other prayer. Even though my mind was foggy, I still remembered most of Kaddish. The images of those metal boxes being wheeled out would haunt my nightmares every night for over a year.

Because my husband could not be there with me, Dr. Abdulateef and his entire team, along with the ICU nurses, became family to me. Dr. Abdulateef spoke with my husband twice a day every day for the entire 20+ days I was in the hospital. He gave him updates and checked on him as well to make sure he was okay. My husband would call the ICU nurses, just before every shift change, to get the overnight and daytime updates on me. The ICU nurses and secretaries never made my husband feel as if he was a bother. They answered all of his questions and gave him more than just the standard update of "she is doing well" or "no change." They went into detail daily because they all knew that family could not be there for the patient.

After I was released from the hospital, my life was still filled with doctor's appointments, uncomfortable medication administrations through the PICC lines, blood tests, x-rays, pinpoint injections, and so much more. The infection and hospital stay not only affected my mouth, but also my blood pressure, memory, speech, swallowing, and more. The prayer for prolonged illness says, "My G~d and G~d of all generations, in my great need I pour out my heart to You. The days and weeks of suffering are hard to endure. In my struggle, let me feel that You are near, a presence whose care enfolds me. Rouse in me the strength to overcome fear and anxiety, and brighten my spirit with the assurance of Your love."

As I slowly recovered, I began to wake up every single day grateful to see a new day. I wanted to not only survive but to thrive. I knew that if I survived and endured the hard days of recovery, my mental energy would lead me to thrive later. I would continue to persist, persevere, carry on, and live!

As time went on, I was incredibly grateful that G~d allowed me to live long enough to see my daughters start their own families. Being able to support my daughter Ruby through her pregnancy was so priceless to me. As I stood in the room at my granddaughter's birth, I was overcome with awe. It was wonderful to shower my daughter with the love and support that my mom was unable to shower on me when I was giving birth. And when I held my newborn granddaughter in my arms, marveling at her tiny features, my heart burst with joy.

I came so close to not being here at this moment, I thought. Not only did I almost die in 2020, but I was ready to throw my life away several times in my younger years. Others told me my life was trash. But now I realized just how precious my life was, and how desperately I wanted to stay alive for every beautiful moment my future may hold.

I wanted to stay alive so I could keep advocating for other hurting women. *I want to be that comforting presence that walks by their side as they bring their babies into the world. I want other women to learn to value their lives and the lives of their families, children, and friends.*

While I was sick, I lost my physical voice: It was hard for me to speak and even swallow. As I healed, I didn't take my voice for granted—literally or metaphorically. I knew that G~d had given me life and health for a reason. He'd given me a voice, and I needed to use it more than ever to speak up about my journey.

My life had an urgent purpose. I knew I had a story to tell, and someone needed to hear it to help them. I continued to soldier on, no matter how hard it was.

Chapter 18

As I recovered, I decided to start checking things off my own bucket list—not just my husband's. He's quite a bit older than me, so I'd prioritized his list of priorities. But now, I started focusing on the things I wanted to do, living my life the way that I wanted to live it. After years of working as a paralegal without an official degree and certification, I got my degree and title.

In addition, I started prioritizing the people who were important to me. I started checking in on my sisters more often and spending time with friends who meant a lot to me. If a friend came to mind, I called them immediately. I wanted them to know that I was thinking about them.

You never know when someone is at a very low point, I reasoned. *You never know when you could save a life. What your call could mean to someone.*

If I think of someone, I immediately pick up the phone and call them. Often, I seem to call them just when something major is going on. My call is much appreciated.

One day, I picked up the phone and called Dr. Sheri Prentiss, the breast cancer survivor.

"I just wanted to call and check in," I told her. "I've been thinking about you and wondering how you are."

Dr. Sheri and I got to talking. Dr. Sheri has such a kind, effervescent personality, and she has a strong faith in God. In the course of our conversation, I told her about my recent bout with illness.

"Now, I take nothing for granted," I told her. "I check in on people and am mindful of individuals."

"That's a wonderful story," said Dr. Sheri. "I can relate to that from my own life. I always tell people in my organization to not only live, but to be bold in their living. Give abundantly. Not just money, but your time, presence, touch, and smile. One time, I met my friend in the cafeteria. I gave her a hug and a smile, but on her way to her car, she dropped dead.

"It wasn't until a few days later when we were planning the memorial service that it dawned on me: *I was the last person to hug her and the last smile she ever saw.*

"Now, I tell individuals, 'I need you to slow down to the point that you realize that the smile you give someone may very well be the last smile they see.' When you take the time to tell someone, 'I want to make sure you're okay,' to talk to her and get her laughing, you can lift her out of the rut. Maybe no one else checked on her that day. Or maybe your voice is the last comforting voice she will ever hear."

"Wow, that's powerful," I said, deeply moved by her story.

"I want you to share on my podcast," Sheri said. "Would you be willing to do that?"

I smiled and nodded simply. "Yes, I would," I said. "I know that this is one of the reasons G~d allowed me to get sick. So I would know just how important every day is. I need to make full use of every day he gives me."

G~d had given me an opportunity to speak on her podcast, allowing even more people to hear my story. And he also opened a door for me in another way I had never expected.

After I got out of the hospital, I wanted to say thank you to the nurses and doctors. If it wasn't for them, I knew I wouldn't be here.

"What should I do to say thank you?" I asked a friend. "If it wasn't for those professionals, I wouldn't be here."

"Lori, what do you do for a living?"

"I don't know. I'm a legal secretary."

She looked at me with a nonverbal rebuke. "Lori, you're a photographer. What can you do with those skills to say thank you?"

"I can do mini family portrait sessions for these doctors, nurses, and their families," I said, finally catching her drift.

So that's what I did.

When I walked into the ICU to invite the doctors to their free photoshoot in Kirby Park, the nurses were pleased.

"A free photo shoot? Count me in," the nurses said. The ICU nurses didn't even realize who I was until we started talking. They just knew I was doing it for free.

"Oh wait, were you in bed twenty-one?"

"Yes, I was."

They looked at me and they said, "Oh my goodness."

I had been so sick, they couldn't even recognize me now. Once they knew who I was, I was surrounded with love. Now that COVID is over, I get hugs and kisses whenever I visit.

"You have truly become part of our family," I told the doctors as I invited them to their free shoot.

I didn't remember most of the doctors, but there was one nurse who sat down and watched TV with me and washed my hair.

"I do remember you," I told her.

"Do you really remember me?"

"I do."

At Kirby Park, the doctors posed in front of lush green grass as the sun slanted through the trees. As I snapped their photos, news cameras snapped mine. I hated the publicity. It was not the reason I was doing it.

But I didn't realize how the PR would continue to help my overall goal of reaching as many people as possible with my story. "Photographer gives back to the healthcare team that treated her," read one headline. "A picture-perfect 'thank you,'" said another. "Care worth a thousand words," a third headline read.

I knew that the PR was a part of the plan. G~d knew that I needed to spread my name, my voice, and my story. I didn't like the publicity, but I knew I'd better get used to it because I have a story to tell. Through my illness, G~d was telling me it was time to get my name and my story out there. It was time to break the stigma.

In November of 2022, I was invited again to speak in my Wilkes-Barre temple. Things were coming full circle. As I overcame my fear of what people thought, the members of my Jewish community were taking their first steps towards overcoming their own fear of change. The first steps toward removing the stigma.

In conclusion, I would like to leave you with two thoughts: Speak Up, and Look to the Future!

Speak Up.

If you have a story to tell, speak up!

For many years, I ran from telling my story because of the shame. I was ashamed of myself and afraid of shaming my family. I ran for many years, but now I stand strong.

Today, I try to live each day as fully as possible. I tell the people in my life—and especially the women I am privileged to meet—that they are not alone. You are not alone. Try and make the best decision possible at any given moment. Be honest with yourself, and with others. Love deeply, love bravely. Do not let the fear of losing those closest to you keep you from loving. Though the road of life may twist and turn, there will always be a chance to start anew and begin living again.

Look to the Future.

There are aspects of my story that are still being written. Even though I have been reunited with my daughter and we have become a family, we're still working on navigating the relationship with Anastasia and her adoptive family. In some ways, we're still working on that full-circle aspect. There will forever be a continuation of this story, learning about myself, and learning about others.

In many ways, my story is just beginning. And so is yours!

When you feel your life is over, remember the messages I shared with my daughter and her gay friend. They are the messages I wish I could have shared with myself as a young, pregnant woman. And they are the messages I want to share with you today.

That's my message to you.

"It will get better."

Yes, it's hard. But even in the darkest moments of pain during our eighteen-year separation, I never regretted walking away from that abortion clinic. I always knew my daughter's life was worth it—and the world is a better place with her in it. Adoption stigma could have led to abortion regrets. I am glad, for me, it didn't. As Tzvi Freeman once said, "If everything were easy, you'd never discover the strength within."

I persevered to who I am today. Twenty years later, I not only speak to other women about being a Jewish Birthmother and my experience with adoption, but I am also a successful business owner of Ceremonies by Lori and ShadowCatcher Photography, LLC. My crowning achievement is having an incredible relationship with my biological children, one I raised and one I placed for adoption.

If I persevered, you can persevere, too.

When life seems really, really bad, it can get better.

My friend Dr. Sheri from Live Today Foundation says that no matter the difficulty, we need to understand that our footsteps are ordered by a loving hand.

"There are some things we can't put an answer to. We just have to accept that all these things are working together for our good. We just have to ask ourselves, 'from this place and this moment on, what good can I get out of this, and what good can I give?'"

Be who you are. You will never be alone. You can find support. You can find someone who is accepting of who you are. You can learn to be accepting of people around you. If your family can't be supportive, then your family is not family. Family doesn't have to be blood. Family can be anyone you choose for it to be.

It does get better.

Trust me, I know from experience.

Made in the USA
Middletown, DE
04 March 2023

26130046R00096